Too often we give ten
women wrestling with
frequently discussions of confessions and catechisms are
written only with an eye to what sets this tradition off from
other denominations. But those tragedies needn't be. How
refreshing to find this pastoral entryway to Christianity
that uses the *Westminster Shorter Catechism* to help the
interested perceive something more of the breadth and
length and height and depth of the love of Christ that
surpasses knowledge. I commend this book to all searching
for something worth living for.

Michael Allen
John Dyer Trimble Professor of Systematic Theology,
Reformed Theological Seminary, Orlando, Florida

This is an invitation to a pleasant conversation about
important matters that can be given to a friend who is
interested in knowing just what it is that Christians believe.
It explains the enduring truths of the Christian faith in
accessible and interesting language that neither talks down
to the reader nor fails to connect with practical concerns we
all have. The author's passion for understanding Christianity
comes through and the discussion of the *Westminster Shorter
Catechism* demonstrates what depths of riches that document
contains. Highly recommended.

Craig Carter
Professor of Theology, Tyndale University, Toronto, Ontario

You may have heard the oft-told story about a little girl who
was afraid to sleep alone during a thunderstorm. Her mom
tried to comfort her, 'Honey, God is right here beside you.

Don't be afraid!' But the little girl wanted more. She said, 'But Mommy, I need God with skin on.' It's a story that illustrates the importance of accessibility. Like that little girl, in one way or another we're all crying out for a God we can understand, converse with, run to, and even touch. And marvel of marvels, in Jesus Christ, God became flesh. Still, to many people there is much about God, the Bible, and Christian truth that seems distant, impersonal, and impractical. Enter Randall Greenwald's book, *Something Worth Living For*. Greenwald takes the classic *Westminster Shorter Catechism*, a seventeenth-century compendium of Christian theology, and makes it accessible to twenty-first-century readers. Through engaging stories, honest reflections, and simple explanations, Greenwald brings the teaching of the Bible on a vast array of topics down to a shelf within reach of both young and old. This book is a needed addition to family and church libraries, to every pastor's study, and to seminary curricula. I will use it as a help in my personal devotions as well as in my teaching ministry. I recommend it highly!

Michael E. Osborne
Dean of Students, Reformed Theological Seminary, Orlando, Florida
Author of *Surviving Ministry*

Pastor Greenwald's *Something Worth Living For* is a fine exposition of the *Westminster Shorter Catechism*. His work is theologically accurate, and he never forgets that he is addressing real people. He reads the Catechism along with them, anticipating the questions that will occur to the reader, even addressing the undefined queasiness that people have when they confront difficult concepts. Randy has a great gift for finding illustrations, real parallels between the deep things of redemption and our present experience. This is the kind of teaching that will move modern people to study the Catechism, and the Scriptures, for themselves.

John Frame
Professor Emeritus of Systematic Theology and Philosophy,
Reformed Theological Seminary, Orlando, Florida

What a gift to the church! Randy Greenwald's book, *Something Worth Living For*, is so needed in the church. It's profound without being pedantic, authentic without being offensive and engaging without compromising the verities of the faith. Finally a book of theology and the Reformed faith that won't bore the reader to death. This is a book that will be such an incredible tool for small study groups, leadership training and laypeople who are often looking for an understandable and useful guide to the Christian faith.

Steve Brown
Founder of Key Life Network and Bible teacher on the national
radio program 'Key Life'
Author of several books

Because Randy and I live on different continents, our friendship has developed almost exclusively through the written word: through e-mails, and through my responding to content on his blog. As a professional writer and editor, I've been consistently impressed by the quality of Randy's writing; I'm also struck by his deep theological knowledge, and how it's paired with genuine pastoral concern for those around him. All three of these traits came together about a dozen years ago, around the time I was returning to the Christian faith, when I wrote Randy to ask him a theological question. Obviously he gave a theologically astute, well-written answer. And just as obviously, he didn't stop there: He pried a bit to find out why I was asking that particular question at that particular time. That led to a much deeper conversation than I wanted about what was going on in my life, but it was a conversation I needed to have and that Randy was happy to provide.

The same qualities I appreciated back then shine through in the draft materials of *Something Worth Living For* that I've read. This is a project that requires writing chops, theological acumen and a pastor's heart. Randy's got them all.

Nathaniel Espino
Founding partner of the Warsaw-based PR agency
Aldgate Strategy Group

Randy Greenwald's *Something Worth Living For* brings the deep, rich, biblical and reformed theology of the seventeenth-century *Westminster Shorter Catechism* to life in the twenty-first century in a way that is warm, inviting, accessible, conversational and centered in Christ and the gospel of saving and transforming grace. I love Randy's refreshing and life-giving approach. I highly recommend this book as a uniquely valuable and much needed new resource for today's church.

Mark Dalbey
President, Covenant Theological Seminary, Creve Coeur,
Missouri

One thing is crystal clear, Christians are not well-prepared for the profound cultural shifts underway in the West. We know we need to be a radically alternative people who 'push as hard as the age that's pushing against us.' But we simply don't know how. Randy Greenwald's *Something Worth Living For* is the help we need to point us back to the ancient paths. This important work will strengthen God's people toward a beautiful orthodoxy that our confused world so desperately needs to see.

Ray Cortese
Senior pastor, Seven Rivers Presbyterian Church, LeCanto, Florida

Catechisms are an ancient and time-tested method that Christians have employed to pass on the core of what they believe about God and what He requires believers to do. Through a simple question-and-answer approach, young and old have been taught biblical truth about our great God and His ways. Randall Greenwald's new discussion of the *Westminster Shorter Catechism*, one of the most treasured of these catechisms, is indeed a welcome tool for exploring the riches of this particular catechism and, even better, for growing in the grace of the Lord Jesus.

Michael A. G. Haykin
Chair & Professor of Church History, The Southern Baptist Theological Seminary, Louisville, Kentucky

Do we really need another book on the *Westminster Shorter Catechism*? It might be tempting to say we don't, since this classic summary of Bible doctrine already has countless summaries and explanations of it in circulation. But both the title and the table of contents of this particular volume immediately captured my imagination. Here is a fresh and thoughtfully applied exploration of the great truths that were first summarised for a distant generation, revisited for today.

Everything about this book, from its tenor and warmth, as much as its content—right through to Randall Greenwald's inviting style—engages readers from every conceivable background. Here's a book that parents could very happily use with their children, or Youth Group leaders with teenagers. It could easily be offered to a friend or colleague who is asking questions about life, or the Christian faith more specifically—either for them to read themselves, or to work through over coffee with them.

It is hard to overstate the enduring worth of this particular catechism, but it is almost as though each generation needs to discover this for themselves. I would heartily commend this guide to the *Shorter Catechism* to anyone who wants to discover what a gem it is for every generation.

Mark Johnston
Minister of Bethel Presbyterian Church, Cardiff, Wales
Author of several books

Randall Greenwald reminds us why a document put together hundreds of years ago is meaningful and valuable in our lives today. Engaging with the *Westminster Shorter Catechism* in a devotional, conversational style, he helps us to delight in who Jesus is and what He has done for His people. In effect, Greenwald helps us read our Bibles better, showing us the landmarks, highways, and terrain so that we can better cruise and delight in the backroad passages of Scripture.

Aimee Byrd
Author of *Theological Fitness* and *No Little Women*

The *Shorter Catechism* is one of those 'treasures in the attic,' as the late Dr. Hughes Old called them, that in more recent years have been re-discovered, brought down into the living room, dusted off, and re-utilized. It is a classic tool for parents who wish to transmit the content and reality of their faith to their children. Part of the dusting off process includes fresh expositions addressed to the living situation of the present generation. Randall Greenwald has done the church the favor of providing that fresh exposition. It will prove to be an effective aid to parents and Sunday school teachers who wish to communicate the gospel to the young people of today.

Terry L. Johnson
Senior minister, Independent Presbyterian Church, Savannah, Georgia

SOMETHING WORTH LIVING FOR

God, the World, Yourself, and the Shorter Catechism

Randall Greenwald

Foreword by Jerram Barrs

Scripture quotations are taken from *The Holy Bible, English Standard Version*, copyright © 2001 by Crossway Bibles, a publishing ministry of Good news Publishers. Used by permission. All rights reserved. ESV Text Edition: 2011.

Copyright © Randall Greenwald 2020

paperback ISBN 978-1-5271-0588-1
epub ISBN 978-1-5271-0665-9
mobi ISBN 978-1-5271-0666-6

Published in 2020
by
Christian Focus Publications Ltd,
Geanies House, Fearn, Ross-shire
IV20 1TW, Scotland
www.christianfocus.com

Cover design by Rubner Durais

Printed and bound by
Bell & Bain, Glasgow

All rights reserved. No part of this publication may be reproduced, stored in a retrieval system, or transmitted in any form or by any means, electronic, mechanical, photocopying, recording or other-wise, without the prior permission of the publisher or a license per-mitting restricted copying. In the U.K. such licenses are issued by the Copyright Licensing Agency, 4 Battlebridge Lane, London, SE1 2HX www.cla.co.uk

CONTENTS

For Tarrik,
And Gabrielle who loves him.

Foreword

Do you believe in God? Are you someone seeking to find out whether God exists or not? Are you in the place of wondering whether God is worth knowing? Do you perhaps struggle with doubts that God is truly good? Are you someone who has been a committed Christian for many years and who knows that you need to keep growing in your faith and in your love for God? Maybe you are someone who has become jaded with the Church, but still feel that you cannot abandon God altogether? Whoever you are; whether you are young, middle aged or old: whatever your convictions, your questions or your doubts are; whether you are a Christian or not; this book is for you.

I did not grow up in a Christian home. In my late teenage years I went through a period of doubt, sadness and despair. But, all through that miserable time I was wrestling with questions about the meaning of life, about whether God exists, about whether God can be trusted if He does indeed exist. Finally, because of the kindness of God, I met someone who answered my questions, encouraged me to express my doubts, and who introduced me to the Bible as the true account of human life and as the answer to my questions and who, eventually, led me to personal faith in Jesus Christ. That someone is still very dear to me fifty-five years later. How I wish that friend, whose name is Michael, could have given me Randall Greenwald's book at that time in my life!

It is a special pleasure to introduce you to this book on the *Westminster Shorter Catechism*, an outstandingly helpful introduction to the Christian faith. Randall Greenwald has written with simplicity and clarity as he unfolds the beauty of the Catechism to us. As we read, we learn what it is to be truly human. We learn who God is and how we can know Him. We discover what God has done in history to come and rescue us from our reluctance to know Him and from our deep disobedience to our human calling. We are taught how God loves us and desires us to love Him; what it means for us to serve and to honor Him in our daily lives; what gifts God has given us to help us walk along this path and how we may come to Him each day through prayer. All this is unfolded for us with wisdom and in easily understandable language.

This book is also written with humility and vulnerability, rare qualities in teachers of the Christian faith. I love the many personal examples Randy gives as he helps us understand the questions and answers of the Catechism. The reader never feels that he or she is being looked down on from on high, or treated as someone who is ignorant and foolish in comparison to the author. Instead, we are invited to learn with Randy, as he continues a life of daily growth, stumbling and falling as he matures in understanding and obedience.

Thank you, Randy, for asking me to write a foreword to this excellent and lovely book. I hope and pray that our Lord and Redeemer, Jesus, will be delighted to use this work in the lives of many, many people for many years to come.

Jerram Barrs
Francis Schaeffer Professor of Apologetics
Senior Scholar of the Francis Schaeffer Institute
Covenant Theological Seminary, St. Louis, Missouri, USA

Preface

What lies behind this book is a lifetime of my own stumbling pursuit after God.

In my late teens formal theology held no interest for me. What I knew about God I knew informally, patched together from Scripture reading, conversations with friends, and, thanks to faithful parents, sitting in church Sunday after Sunday. I knew enough about the Bible to make theological claims, but I had no way of testing the accuracy of those claims against the long history and the reasoned depth of theological reflection and formulation.

At that stage I was, like many in that position, ripe to be hijacked. I had knowledge but no roots and would have been easy prey for those who champion movements that have enough truth to seem plausible but which are full of error and falsehood. That many are, at that point, sucked into such movements is the cause of much grief. But it is probably a more common sadness that such a person may simply stall in his growth and be stunted in his understanding. Christianity is a generational faith. Its riches are passed down from generation to generation. When I tapped into the resources and truths prepared and enjoyed by my forefathers, I found great treasure.

In college I stumbled upon a church whose preacher presented Scripture with a then unfamiliar warmth, depth, and life.[1] Soon thereafter I was directed by a professor to the book, *Knowing God*, by British theologian J. I. Packer.[2] Packer introduced me to a God who was at once bigger than I could conceive and more loving than I could possibly accept. Packer's writing was deeply biblical and warmly engaging. Without my knowing it, I was being invited to drink deeply of theology. It was becoming a pathway, a road toward that elusive 'personal relationship with Christ' that so many of my friends had spoken of but none could define.

Unknowingly, but happily, I was being exposed to the outlines of *Reformed* theology. When someone pushed me to go deeper at this point, my first impulse, as it is for many, was to run. My mind and heart initially recoiled at what I did not understand. That did not last long. Through the patient teaching of dear friends, I began to see the heart of the Reformed tradition and the richness and comfort it afforded. I began to realize that this was the tradition informing the preaching of my church in East Lansing and the pen of Dr Packer.

When the pieces began to come together for me, my heart was 'strangely warmed,' to steal a phrase from John Wesley. I have ever since tried to convey this warmth to others. To help others sense the freedom, awe, and security

---

1   The Reverend Willard E. Michael, then the pastor of East Lansing Trinity Church in East Lansing, Michigan.

2   J. I. Packer, *Knowing God* (United States: InterVarsity Press, 1973, 1993).

that knowing God through the lens of Reformed theology brings is my passion. This book is an outgrowth of that passion.

I cannot recall when I was first introduced to the beauty of the language of the *Westminster Shorter Catechism*. Packer's reference to the answer to Q/A #4 in *Knowing God* was perhaps my first serious encounter with it. Over the years I have come to love this brief but compelling tool. Weighing in at 107 questions may not count for many as 'brevity,' but there is an economy of language in these questions and answers which remarkably captures the essential elements of historic Christianity viewed from within the Reformed tradition.

I have since urged others more qualified and gifted to write a modern and engaging presentation of the content of the Catechism. That they have not taken on the challenge has left it to me. I have done so with the prayer that there may be a reader, somewhere, who may sense, for the first time perhaps, the warmth and beauty that is Reformed theology. My hope is that he or she might be moved to find here just what it means to enjoy a living and vital relationship with the living, gracious, and holy God of our salvation.

Introduction

A Word to the Curious

In writing this book, I'm assuming that you are curious. Maybe you are in a church that has some relationship with the *Westminster Shorter Catechism* and you want to know more about what your church believes. Perhaps you have seen the Catechism[1] mentioned somewhere and wonder what it is about. I write to satisfy those curiosities, of course.

But there are deeper curiosities. It's possible that you are curious about the beliefs of Christianity itself. The Catechism, being a summary of basic, historic Christian doctrine, is a good place to begin. My hope is that you will have your curiosity stimulated by this book to dig even more deeply into what you discover here.

For some of you, life has shaken you. You once held to some form of a Christian faith, but now you are older and you wonder what happened to that. Perhaps your understanding of Christianity has been challenged by Christians behaving badly or by Christianity being handled poorly in the public sphere. You are reading this, perhaps,

---

1 Any time the word 'catechism' is capitalized, I am referring to the *Westminster Shorter Catechism*.

because you are trying to recapture the faith you once held. I welcome you. I understand where you are.

Mostly I hope you are curious about God. If this book can help readers like you know God better, then the effort of writing and reading will have been worth it.

Structurally, this book is a collection of reflections centered on the 107 questions and answers of the *Westminster Shorter Catechism*. I picture us sitting on a porch or at a coffee shop discussing the issues the Catechism raises in the order it raises them. Though intending to be theologically accurate this is not meant to be academic. The goal of my comments is to encourage your thoughtful and devotional engagement with the Christian faith as it is expressed in the Catechism. I want you to not just know what the Catechism says about God, the world, and yourself. I want to encourage you to reflect on its meaning and implications.

To this end, it is important to let the logic of the Catechism lead us. It is important to begin at the beginning and to move thoughtfully to the end. There is no rush. It is okay to read one section per day, or less frequently, if that is most comfortable for you. Each is short enough to be read quickly, but substantive enough to encourage reflection.

What is a Catechism?

To become familiar with this world called the *Westminster Shorter Catechism* it would be good to walk around it a bit and clarify what we are dealing with.

HISTORY

The familiar 'Alphabet Song' in which the English alphabet is recited to the tune of 'Twinkle, Twinkle Little Star' is a teaching tool to help children learn and retain fundamental knowledge of the alphabet. A catechism shares a similar goal. Using a question and answer format, a catechism is a teaching tool designed to present and preserve fundamental theological knowledge in a way that is accessible and easily retained. The Protestant Reformation of the sixteenth century stirred a renewal and recovery of a deeply biblical and historic Christianity that needed to be taught and preserved. Consequently, many confessions and catechisms were produced during that era as means to that end. The *Westminster Shorter Catechism* was one of the last, and one of the most enduring, of those tools. It has had a deep impact upon generations of Christians.

The *Westminster Shorter Catechism* traces its history to England in the early 1600s. King Charles I, in need of resources to fund a war, was forced by that need to call a meeting of Parliament. This Parliament, not favorable to the king, used the occasion to rebel against the monarchy and to implement a more republican form of government. In those days it was commonly thought that to have a government one must have a church, and to have a church one must have a foundational statement of beliefs. Thus the rebellion against the king corresponded with a desire to reform and purify the church.

To produce a confession for the new republic and the new church, Parliament summoned 120 'divines'—scholars and clergymen from throughout England, together with some non-voting contributors from Ireland and Scotland—to create a confession of faith corresponding to the commitments of the new government. These men (for they were, in fact, all men) met and deliberated for several years in the Jerusalem Chamber of Westminster Abbey[2] in London, producing, among other things, a doctrinal statement (the *Westminster Confession of Faith*) and two catechisms. One of these, the *Westminster Larger Catechism*, was a lengthy catechism intended to guide preachers in their teaching. The other, the *Westminster Shorter Catechism*, the document with which we are concerned, was designed to be used by members of the church, by families, and by children, to guide them into an understanding of sound doctrine.

The use of these documents, given their final form in the later years of the 1640s, was short-lived in England. When the monarchy was restored in 1660, the Confession and Catechisms were quickly laid aside. But not so in Scotland. There, adopted by the Church of Scotland, their influence was significant. When those influenced by the Confession and Catechisms arrived in the colonies of the Americas, they brought these documents with them for use in their churches. So it was that the Westminster Confession and Catechisms came to define the accepted doctrine of Presbyterian churches in the United States.[3]

CHARACTER

A catechism is a distillation of great truths for preservation and learning. And yet how does one reasonably distill the

---

2   Which lent its name to the documents the assembly produced there.

3   I should note that the *Confession of Faith* was adopted in America with some changes, particularly with regard to its teaching on the relationship between church and state. Such modification was not needed in this, the *Shorter Catechism*.

vast knowledge that is found in the Bible in such a way that neither cheapens the whole nor omits critical parts? To create, for example, a concise yet accurate definition of God seems impossible. God cannot be distilled. But if we ask, 'What information about God does a Christian, particularly a child or a recent convert, need to know?' the answer is more accessible. A catechism, therefore, does not pretend to say everything that could be said. What it does say is sufficient to orient someone to the Christian faith in such a way that protects him from false teaching and enables him to appreciate and worship the true God with depth.

Both of these things mattered to those who composed the Catechism. They wanted this document to serve both truth and worship. They wanted those taught by it to be solidly grounded and protected from falsehood. They also wanted to produce worshipers whose passion and devotion matched their own.

The story is told that when the Westminster Assembly was wrestling with an adequate answer to the question of God, frustration led them to break for a time of prayer. The Scottish commissioner, Samuel Rutherford, was asked to pray, and it is said he prayed, 'O God, you who are infinite, eternal, and unchangeable in your wisdom, power, holiness, goodness, and truth….' The language of this prayer was captured as the famous answer to the question 'What is God?' Whether this story is true or not, it accurately illustrates the devotion infusing the Catechism as a whole. It was produced by men who knew and loved God and who wanted clarity in the essentials of the faith to lead others to know, love, worship, and enjoy the God whom they knew, loved, worshiped, and enjoyed. They succeeded with a clarity and a beauty that few if any could match today.

STRUCTURE

That the writers of the Catechism clearly loved order is revealed in its inherent logic. The first question and answer sets the tone and direction for the whole. The second teaches that the foundation for all our knowledge of God is found in the Bible. The third then divides that revealed knowledge into two broad categories. The first of these—what we are to know concerning God—is developed in questions four through thirty-eight. Attention then turns to the duty which God requires of us, developed in questions thirty-nine through one hundred and seven. This latter section includes a practical exposition of the Ten Commandments and a thoughtful reflection on the content of the Lord's Prayer.

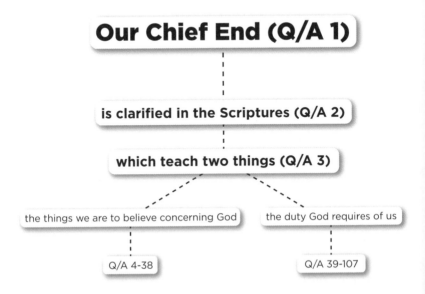

Our Chief End (Q/A 1)

is clarified in the Scriptures (Q/A 2)

which teach two things (Q/A 3)

the things we are to believe concerning God

the duty God requires of us

Q/A 4-38

Q/A 39-107

The Catechism is not perfect, of course. It reflects, as any such document must, the concerns of the men who wrote it. It has received criticism for bringing too little emphasis to the Holy Spirit and for being too dogmatic in its application of the Ten Commandments, concerns we will address in due course. As well, being a document true to its time, it may seem like women did not exist. The chief end of 'man' is considered in the first question, and this masculine tone permeates the whole. No harm or exclusion is meant by that. It was the language convention of the time, nothing more. I try to reflect in my comments that the idea of 'man' does in fact include women.

Some find the language obscure and have made efforts to update it. I resist that because I find the precision and force of the original English hard to surpass. Any attempt to re-write it only lessens it. That said, I have made two changes to the actual text of the Catechism. First, I have removed the archaic spellings. 'Hath' has become 'has' and 'continueth' 'continues,' and so forth. This changes nothing other than making the words conform to modern spelling and pronunciation. Secondly, when Scripture is quoted, as it is throughout the section on the Ten Commandments, I have replaced the Authorized Version of 1611 used by the authors with a modern translation, the English Standard Version, as this is more likely to be the one being read by the audience for whom I write.

The Catechism may feel foreign to readers more familiar with 'Calvin and Hobbes' than with John Calvin. It demands of us more thought than that required by the latest internet meme or Twitter rant. There is rich gold to be mined here, and always the search for gold requires effort. My intention is to help you dig.

The pastors and scholars who created this Catechism were motivated by a deep passion for God and for His people. They—like those who before them translated the Bible into English—took great risks so that they might remove '…the barrier between learned and unlearned by making Christianity fully intelligible in the common languages.'[4] This book does not reach the level of what they accomplished, and the only risk I run is that readers won't like it. And yet I, too, want to make 'Christianity fully intelligible in [today's] common languages.' I want to bring the riches of this Catechism before you in a way that both satisfies and further whets your curiosity. I will judge this successful if, when finished, you love God just a bit more and are moved more deeply to glorify and enjoy Him.

Oh come, let us worship and bow down;
let us kneel before the LORD, our Maker!
For he is our God,
and we are the people of his pasture,
and the sheep of his hand.[5]

---

4 Marilynne Robinson, *The Givenness of Things* (United States: HarperCollins, 2015), pp. 19-20.

5 Psalm 95:6-7.

Part 1
Something Worth Believing

This first part of the Catechism teaches us theology—what we are to know about God. And some of you in hearing that have an impulse to run. The very word 'theology' stirs difficult emotions. I want to urge you to not bolt. Not yet.

Years ago a poster circulated around our church. Beneath a drawing of the Peanuts cartoon dog Snoopy, with his paws outstretched, was a caption that said, 'Hugs. Not theology.' As the pastor—that is, the one paid to teach theology to those passing around the poster—I had to work hard not to take that personally. Nevertheless, I understood it. It revealed the deep human longing for community we all feel. We really do want a hug.

It also revealed the popular notion that theology gets in the way of community. And it does sometimes. You perhaps have experienced those using their theology to feel superior to others. Or you have seen theology used as a tool inappropriately to divide Christian from Christian. So, yes, in this case, hugs trump theology every time.

And yet the misuse of a thing need not keep us from it. Good things are prone to misuse. My daughter Adria once took her violin bow and whacked her brother Seth because, in her judgment, he was being annoying. Diverted from its purpose as an instrument of beauty, it broke. It was not meant to be a weapon. Neither is theology.

The Catechism unveils the ancient, historic understanding of God and His creation, of God's covenant with His people, and of God's Redeemer and His work. In this way it presents theology. And not everyone will accept these historic Christian ideas. So on the one hand, theology necessarily draws lines and makes distinctions. But clarity itself on these matters is not a bad thing. Good theology well expressed can help us understand one another, where we agree and where we differ, and understanding is the first step toward relationship. Further, good theology well taught warms our hearts toward God and can massage our hearts to have compassion toward others. Good theology, I hope to show, can in fact lead to hugs.

As well, good theology leads to song.

Poet Kathleen Norris suggests 'we go to church in order to sing, and theology is secondary.'[1] True, the desire to form and be in community moves us toward one another ('hugs'), and together the impulse is to sing, something we are rarely able to do with others. But is theology secondary? Good theology gives us the content of our song.

My desire for the chapters that follow is to unfold for you a theology that invites you to stay, and to sing.

1 Kathleen Norris, *Dakota: A Spiritual Geography* (United States: Ticknor and Fields, 1993), p. 91.

1

The Journey's End

Journeys always start at their end, not at their beginning.

When I stand up from the chair in which I am sitting, it is because I have some place to go or some task to accomplish. My first step and all subsequent steps are determined by the end on which I've already decided. That end could be good or bad, worthy or unworthy. It could be to get a cup of coffee or to drop out of school. But journeys always begin with the end.

An end that motivates us to begin the journey of a formal study of theology may simply be to know more. To learn more about the Christian faith is a good and worthy end. The Catechism, though, pushes us to consider a deeper, more profound end, an end that impacts far more than just the study of theology. This end is linked to who we are and who God is and it will set the tone for our journey through the Catechism. And if we understand it, it will also set the tone for our journey through life.

1 LIVING FOR GOD'S GLORY

> Q. 1. What is the chief end of man?
> A. Man's chief end is to glorify God, and to enjoy him forever.

'Hey! Hello in there. Hey! What's so important? What you got here that's worth living for?'

So shouts Miracle Max at the mostly dead (but slightly alive) Westley in Rob Reiner's classic movie, *The Princess Bride*. Though this is a wonderfully fun and playful movie, the question about what one finds worth living for is a terribly serious one. It is pondered by philosophers and lovers, by visionaries and artists, and, at some level, by everyone. What makes life worthwhile? Or, as the Catechism puts it, what is the chief end, the ultimate purpose, of life? What do we have that's worth living for?

We all have an answer, conscious or not, of some sort. The college student may live to graduate, perhaps to find a spouse or pursue a lifelong career ambition. The homeless family may live only to find the next meal. The salesman may live for the next deal and the addict the next hit. Some live to find the approval their fathers never gave them. Others live to achieve a renown so far deprived them. Some live to get as much pleasure as they can before they die, others as much power. Few articulate what drives them. They just 'know' at some level that the happiness they seek resides somewhere beyond their reach, and they pursue it. This thing pursued is our end, our purpose, and our goal.

In a sense, this end is in fact our god.

In the early days of my parenting what mattered to me, I am ashamed to say, was my reputation as a pastor. I parented my children concerned not by what was best for them or even what was scripturally sound but by what served best my reputation as a 'good pastor.' My chief end, one might say, was to bring glory to my name and enjoy my reputation forever. This was never expressed and was never conscious. Yet this was the goal which drove me. It was the inadequate and unworthy god whom I served.

That thing for which we live is our god, and if we cherish the wrong god, an inadequate and false one, then serving that god will enslave us and lead us to disappointment.[1] Only when we serve and cherish the true and living God will we find the joy and purpose for which we were created. Our chief and ultimate purpose, the only one that will not disappoint, is to live for the glory of God, and, in the end, to find our ultimate and complete enjoyment in Him.

To develop the implications of this is the aim of the remaining questions and answers of the Catechism.

One shaped by a pursuit of God's glory will bend every part of his life to that end. Johann Sebastian Bach inscribed at the bottom of many of his great musical manuscripts the initials 'SDG,' a Latin symbol meaning 'to the glory of God alone.' That should be inscribed on every burger we grill and every email we send.

---

1   A very helpful discussion of this is found in *Counterfeit Gods: The Empty Promises of Money, Sex, and Power, and the Only Hope that Matters* by Tim Keller (United States: Dutton, 2009).

Living for God's glory is the posture out of which people will find their greatest happiness. It is also the posture against which the deepest part of us tends to rebel. We prefer to think of ourselves as the masters of our own universe, which leads us to reject the claim of God over us, even if that claim comes as kindness.

It is the beauty of the biblical story outlined for us in the Catechism that God does not leave such rebels to their own chosen misery. He shows mercy to us in our rebellion, a mercy culminating in our being made 'perfectly blessed in the full enjoying of God to all eternity.'[2]

It is the knowledge of this mercy alone that can soften our cold, hard, rebellious hearts and replace them with hearts eager to see the glory of God alone as the one thing worth living for.[3]

2 LIVING BY GOD'S WORD

> *Q. 2. What rule has God given to direct us how we may glorify and enjoy him?*
> *A. The Word of God, which is contained in the Scriptures of the Old and New Testaments, is the only rule to direct us how we may glorify and enjoy him.*

---

2   Readers should note that the 'chief end' includes enjoying God as well as glorifying Him. This critical aspect of our fundamental purpose, of that which gives life fullness and meaning both in this life and the next, will be touched upon more fully in our reflection upon Q/A 38 of the Catechism.

3   Aiming us in this direction, the Apostle Paul says: 'So, whether you eat or drink, or whatever you do, do all to the glory of God' (1 Cor. 10:31).

> Q. 3. What do the Scriptures principally teach?
> A. The Scriptures principally teach what man is to believe concerning God, and what duty God requires of man.

Many metaphors have been proposed by which we can understand the place of the Bible in our lives. The Catechism here speaks of it as a 'rule'—a guide to how we ought to act and think regarding God. This rule is found in the whole Bible, Old and New Testaments alike. Psalm 119 uses words similar to 'rule' such as 'law,' 'promise,' and 'precept.' Elsewhere it is called the 'Word of God,' and as it is written it is called 'Scripture.'

None of these images are as graphic as that which is used by the biblical book of Hebrews. There we read that the Word of God is 'sharper than any two-edged sword,' capable of exposing the hidden truths of the human heart[4] with surgical precision.

Allowed to come near, such a sword can reveal things deep and hidden within us, things we want to hide from others and which we may not want to know about ourselves. It can expose our nakedness before God and our vulnerability to sin. Since such exposure can be frightening, we attempt to keep this sword in its sheath when we can. We dull its edge as much as we are able, nursing it to say soft and safe things. We will avoid its hard parts, and we will not let it come too

---

4   'For the word of God is living and active, sharper than any two-edged sword, piercing to the division of soul and of spirit, of joints and of marrow, and discerning the thoughts and intentions of the heart' (Heb. 4:12).

close because we prefer to keep our thoughts and intentions hidden. Sharp things scare us.

And yet, sharp things in skilled hands can bring blessing. Our children would allow a sharp needle to prick their skin to dislodge a splinter. Though painful, when in the hands of their mother, they let it come near. In the hands of a skilled surgeon, knives are healing things. This two-edged sword we know as the Bible is the Word of a loving and kind Father. In the hands of any other this would be frightening. To see that it is in His hands changes everything.

This, though, requires that we be convinced that Scripture *is* the Word of God. There are many things to commend the Bible to us as trustworthy—its beauty, its internal consistency, and its external correspondence to life as we know it. But the only way to know that this is the Word from God is to trust the Bible's own claim to be so. The God who is true has spoken, and a part of what He has spoken is that this is His book. All that is in it supports this claim, but ultimately, we believe the Bible to be the Word from God because that is what it says about itself. To believe God is to believe His Word.

And yet this Word of God was written by men. Over a span of 1,500 years God so guided the lives of dozens of men that what they wrote, reflecting their own unique context and style, was exactly what God wanted to have written. It is this Word of God that alone can teach us how we might glorify and enjoy Him, and so we study it closely and treasure it deeply. Though it may cut, it cuts for our healing and growth. Such a sword is to be welcomed.

A friend, who grew up in rural Manatee County, Florida, once told me that he would just as soon be without his pants as without his pocket knife. Ignoring the conundrum that a pocket knife would have no home on a man without pants, his point was made. The usefullness of the knife was so diverse that he could not imagine not having it readily available. Handled poorly, or if it were dull, the knife could do great harm. But treated with respect, and kept near and with frequent use, it is a gift.

Such is the Bible. It is a thing full of beauty, of truth, of wisdom, of challenge, of heartbreak, and of hope. With the psalmist we come praying that God would teach us wonderful things from it.[5] Even if it makes us bleed.

---

5   'Open my eyes, that I may behold
     wondrous things out of your law' (Ps. 119:18).

2

The Greatness of God

Perhaps the most radical contribution of the Catechism to human thinking is this insistence that God is to be first in our thinking and doing. That He is humanity's chief end and joy is not a common idea in the university or in philosophical or political discourse. It is rarely suggested as a consideration in our economic or parenting decisions. So much around us implicitly and explicitly shapes our thinking in a different direction that we meet this idea as strange or quaint or rather odd. Ingrained ideas do not easily change.

For this way of thinking to take root we must come to know something about this God who claims this central place in our lives. Who is it whose glory is to be our chief end? This is the direction in which the Catechism now moves. Maybe we will like Him and maybe we will not, but we must know Him as He is revealed to us and not as we might imagine Him to be. Our whole dealing will then be with the God revealed in the Bible. It is essential that we be clear who and what He is.

This may require our minds to be stretched. In some cases, a lot. But it is an essential step.

3 WHAT GOD IS

> Q. 4. What is God?
> A. God is a spirit, infinite, eternal, and unchangeable, in his being, wisdom, power, holiness, justice, goodness and truth.

The pastor and author Frederick Buechner asks us to imagine a situation in which one night God swirls the stars in the Milky Way arranging them to spell, 'God is!'[1] People would look up and there would be the proof all had been seeking. The result would be immediate and dramatic, Buechner suggests. Churches would suddenly overflow and the entire religious conversation would be shifted.

But Buechner is missing something. Thoughtful people would still be left questioning. '*What* is God?' What is it that '*is*?' We think that we know 'what' such a god is. But without any other information we would still tend to shape the reality to which this word in the stars points as one that conforms to our pre-existing prejudices. To overcome those prejudices and to give us a clear understanding, God must tell us more about Himself than what two words in the sky could do. This God has done.

The Catechism has distilled all that we are taught about God in the Bible's sixty-six books into eighteen audacious words.

---

1   Frederick Buechner, *The Magnificent Defeat* (United States: HarperOne, 1985) 'The Message in the Stars', pp. 44-5.

This God who 'is' is an infinite, eternal, and unchangeable spirit. He has no beginning and no end. He possesses no borders in time or space. He has no body and is not subject to change, growth, or decay. The 'what' of God is spirit.

But this spirit that is God is a 'who.' He bears, like us, profoundly personal attributes. He is wise, bearing complete and sufficient knowledge and perfection of judgment that arises from knowing all things. He has all power without limit, and He is the very definition of purity. In all that He does, He acts with fairness out of a deep, deep well of goodness and love. In Him dwells all that can be known, without error. And He can never lie.

This God, being personal, can be known by us. The Bible's presentation of God is by no means as arid and clinical as these eighteen words might suggest. He is revealed as a father, as a shepherd, and as a redeemer. He is a mother hen gathering her chicks beneath her wings, and He is a warrior fighting to set His people free. The Catechism speaks of who God is in Himself. But it is in relationship that we come to love Him.

We come to love Him, and if we are honest, to be troubled by Him. This God, in His infinite, eternal, and unchangeable wisdom does things we cannot comprehend and denies to us things we are persuaded we cannot do without. He acts in ways that mystify and anger us. He reveals Himself as He is and invites us to trust Him. If He is real, then He will—like any other real person—act in ways that puzzle us. If the god we embrace never makes us uncomfortable, then we can be sure that we have shaped Him in our own image[2]

---

2   This insight is from Tim Keller. He speaks it often in various places.

and not as He is. In spite of the depth of His revelation and the thoroughness of our study of Him, there will always remain things we do not understand and truth we cannot comprehend. But what we can know is rich, and what we come to know draws us to Him.

The stars already point to the existence of God. The whole creation points to Him. Many have already read the message there. 'God is,' they declare. But it is left for God to speak that we might know what and who He is. Gratefully, He has not remained silent.

4 HOW GOD IS

> Q. 5. Are there more Gods than one?
> A. There is but one only, the living and true God.

> Q. 6. How many persons are there in the Godhead?
> A. There are three persons in the Godhead; the Father, the Son, and the Holy Ghost; and these three are one God, the same in substance, equal in power and glory.

I

There are many things my brain cannot comprehend that others seem to grasp with no problem. Quantum mechanics is one of those. How something as complex as a human being develops from a single cell is another. I can't seem to understand how a heavy airplane is kept in the air by two relatively slender wings, how waves form on the beach, or how to explain the origin of a parent's love.

And yet, for all those things there are people who *do* understand them. It is even possible that with enough help and study, I could understand them as well. But of the essential nature of the true God which we have come to understand by the word 'Trinity,' the most any of us can do is to do our best to describe what is revealed and to accept the fact that full understanding is hidden in the consciousness of the infinite and eternal God.

And yet, though we cannot *fully* understand, God has been a good and patient teacher. He has used time as an ally in revealing to people the fullness of His being.

When He walked with Adam and Eve in the garden in the cool of the day,[3] or spoke to Abraham,[4] or appeared to Moses in the burning bush,[5] He communicated who He was in a way that could be understood. He came as a singular God, as one whom people should fear and trust, as one living and true. In contrast to the notions of many other people groups who imagined a plethora of gods—gods of fertility, gods of war, gods of passion—God taught His people to affirm that He is one God,[6] and that his name is 'I Am.'[7]

---

3   'And they heard the sound of the LORD God walking in the garden in the cool of the day...' (Gen. 3:8).

4   'Now the LORD said to Abram, "Go from your country and your kindred and your father's house to the land that I will show you"' (Gen. 12:1).

5   'God called to him out of the bush, "Moses, Moses!"' (Exod. 3:4).

6   'Hear, O Israel: The LORD our God, the LORD is one' (Deut. 6:4).

7   'God said to Moses, "I AM WHO I AM." And he said, "Say this to the people of Israel: I AM has sent me to you"' (Exod. 3:14).

This, in itself, is a truth which humans sometimes find hard to digest. Many religious cultures still affirm a pantheon of gods, and in the West it is common to imagine that everyone's conception of God is equally valid. If everyone's contradictory idea of God is accepted as true, then there is really no true God at all.

And yet there is a God, the living and true God, and He revealed Himself to Israel as one. Those who called Him their God had no question on that point. His people came to love Him as the only true God with all their heart, soul, and might,[8] and He loved them back as shepherd, protector, and king. He is one.

II

And then Jesus came bearing the fullness of God's attributes. He called Himself a Son, referred to and spoke to God as His Father. He did and claimed things that only God could do or claim. He spoke of Himself in ways that echoed the divine name 'I Am.'[9] And He, this Son, promised when He was gone to send one whom He called the Comforter, the Spirit of the Father and the Son. When He, the Son, died and rose from the dead because death could not hold Him, He commissioned the Church, whom He had formed, to

---

8   'You shall love the LORD your God with all your heart and with all your soul and with all your might' (Deut. 6:5).

9   'Jesus said to them, "Truly, truly, I say to you, before Abraham was, I am"' (John 8:58).

admit others through baptism in the name of these three, the Father, the Son, and the Holy Spirit.[10]

What were these monotheists, these believers in one God, supposed to do with all of this? Were they to affirm three gods after all? Is there one god appearing in different forms at different times? Is there one god who has created and sent forth lower beings to represent him? Though each of these (erroneous) ideas has been embraced in some way and continue to form the foundational teaching of many non-orthodox sects, such solutions have not been acceptable to the wise, careful, and broad history of the Church.

Finding the right language to give expression to what Scripture teaches by way of revelation has proven difficult. There is one God. The Father is God, the Son is God, and the Spirit is God. Historic Christian theology eventually found it necessary to use the language of 'persons' within the 'godhead' to establish the parameters by which God could be spoken of and described. There is one God and there are three persons in God. Each person is the same in substance, equal in power and glory. One is not a part of the other, but each is wholly God.

III

And we can say little more. That we cannot logically embrace three that are one does not make it any less true. What we can embrace is the beauty that the Trinity reveals, for life would be sterile without it.

---

10 'Go therefore and make disciples of all nations, baptizing them in the name of the Father and of the Son and of the Holy Spirit...' (Matt. 28:19).

Of the many things the Bible teaches us about God, the most comforting to many is that He is 'love.'[11] But what is love if God is a mere unity? Love by its nature is delight in and commitment to another, and without another on whom that love is placed, it is a mere abstraction. Love requires, if we may say it this way, a plurality of persons. That God could love us and receive our love required our creation. But for God to *be* love, for love to be a part of His eternal and infinite being, does not require our creation. He has always been love. Within the godhead there has always been delight, affection, and devotion. God is love because God is Trinity.

When we are invited into relationship with this God, we are not entering into something that is new for Him, but something that is eternally a part of who He has always been. The wonder of the love that we have for God and that He gives to us is that we, by this, are welcomed into something eternally wonderful.[12] To be a Christian means to be welcomed into an experience of God Himself. We are loved and can love God, because He is love and always has been love.

Our God is a relational being who does not need us, but welcomes us. Though this, too, is beyond my ability to understand, it is something my heart thrills to know.[13]

---

11 'Anyone who does not love does not know God, because God is love' (1 John 4:8). 'God is love, and whoever abides in love abides in God, and God abides in him' (1 John 4:16).

12 '...that which we have seen and heard we proclaim also to you, so that you too may have fellowship with us; and indeed our fellowship is with the Father and with his Son Jesus Christ' (1 John 1:3).

13 A wonderful little book discussing the practical implications of the Trinity is Michael Reeves's *Delighting in the Trinity: An Introduction*

5 What God Does

> Q. 7. What are the decrees of God?
> A. The decrees of God are his eternal purpose, according to the counsel of his will, whereby, for his own glory, he has foreordained whatsoever comes to pass.

> Q. 8. How does God execute his decrees?
> A. God executes his decrees in the works of creation and providence.

Occasionally, when a celebrity is awarded an honor, she will thank her parents, her agent, and maybe her lucky stars. And sometimes she thanks God.

But did God have anything to do with it?

The Bible is clear that there is a way in which nothing in all creation and history is random. All happens according to God's wise care, the counsel of His will. The Bible places no limits to God. There is no ounce of earth, no segment of time, no point in the universe that lies outside His rule. The Bible ascribes to Him all kinds of glorious acts, from the blossoming of a rose[14] to the resurrection of Jesus.[15] It ascribes to Him as well all manner of horrors including

---

to the Christian Faith (United States: InterVarsity Press, 2012).

14 Consider here Jesus' reflections on how God 'clothes' the flowers with beauty in Matthew 6:25-34.

15 'This Jesus God raised up, and of that we all are witnesses' (Acts 2:32).

the cross on which His son died.[16] He has 'foreordained whatsoever comes to pass'[17] to the end that the knowledge of His glory may cover the earth as the waters cover the sea.[18] As the children's song goes, 'There's nothing our God cannot do.' That is biblical truth.

When such thoughts were first presented to me as an eighteen-year-old college student, I found such thinking troubling. I struggled, as do many, with the thought that if these things were true then people must be no more than robots, mechanically acting out a horrifying script upon an elaborate stage. So deeply did this trouble me that I tried to put distance between myself and those sharing it with me.

But I continued to attend church. And though this way of thinking about God's rule, His sovereignty, was not made much of in my church, the Bible was. It was read, and the more I heard it read, the more this vision of the greatness and sovereignty of God grew. The Bible seemed to feel none of the tension that I felt. Humans in the Bible were free. They made real choices. They genuinely felt love and hate and envy and compassion. They pursued their dreams and laid down their lives for others. And though in some sense beyond our comprehension their lives were foreordained, they felt no constraint. As the Bible was read to me then and as I've continued to read it, I hear stories of real people

---

16 '...this Jesus, delivered up according to the definite plan and foreknowledge of God, you crucified and killed by the hands of lawless men' (Acts 2:23).

17 For language similar to this language of the Catechism, see Ephesians 1:11: '...him who works all things according to the counsel of his will ....'

18 'For the earth will be filled with the knowledge of the glory of the LORD as the waters cover the sea' (Hab. 2:14).

living real lives with no evidence that such living conflicts with anything in the sovereign counsel of God.

Sometimes our theological musings drain the beauty from a truth. We take things meant to be a comfort and harden them into a sterile doctrine. This idea of the sovereign foreordination of God ought not to be held with such sterility. Difficult as this idea may seem, our hearts long to know that everything is going to be all right, and the only way to know that is to know that there is a God of sovereign rule who guides human affairs.

Yes, we still have questions about this. But God has not revealed what He has revealed to answer all our questions. He has revealed what He has revealed so that we might trust Him. Knowing His sovereignty (along with His infinite goodness), we can know that the profoundly troubling things that happen are not the random outworkings of an impersonal universe intent on killing us, or even the mere evidence of human wickedness. They *are* these things, but they are not *merely* these things. They are at the same time a part of a universe that is never without purpose and never without meaning. There is meaning I am never meant to know or understand. Yet, what comes to pass comes to pass only by the divine will of the good God. Only because He is good and powerful can we know that '...neither death nor life, nor angels nor rulers, nor things present nor things to come, nor powers, nor height nor depth, nor anything else in all creation, will be able to separate us from the love of God in Christ Jesus our Lord.'[19]

---

19 Romans 8:38-9.

6 THE BEAUTY OF CREATION

> Q. 9. What is the work of creation?
> A. The work of creation is God's making all things of nothing, by the word of his power, in the space of six days, and all very good.

My son, Colin, once persuaded me to read a book about string theory—a theoretic probing into the nature of the physical world around us seeking the fundamental building block of all matter. The author backed up his arguments with eleven-dimensional math. Though little of this made sense to me, it did cause me to remember the profound complexity of creation. Creation, beautiful and complex, stirs wonder and pushes us to consider the Creator, the one who made all things, including the stuff out of which all things are made. All creation tilts our wonder toward the Creator. Even the most neutral observer will at times speak of the design of nature. It's hard to escape the sense that a designer lies behind it all.

On this most Christians agree. Disagreements lie in the details. Reflecting the language of Scripture, the Catechism tells us God created all there is in six days. Some believe this to speak of six ordinary twenty-four-hour days. Others, equally committed to Scripture, read this as speaking of long periods of time. Still others contend that scientific or temporal precision was not at all a concern of the original author.

Pressing further, some contend that the earth is not much more than six thousand years old. Others argue that the idea that science has proven an ancient earth is not incompatible with the Bible. There will be a day when all will agree, but it is not now.

In the meantime, we must not lose sight of this: *both* Scripture and creation reveal truth about God. Both are the work of His hands and declare His glory.[20] There can be no conflict, ultimately, between God's revelation in Scripture and that seen in nature, as there is no division or double-speak in God.

Any apparent conflict arises from either a misinterpretation of the data of nature or a misreading of Scripture. When Scripture is clear, then we need to entertain the idea that we are misinterpreting what we see in nature. When what we see in nature is indisputable, we need to consider how we might be misreading Scripture.

And when there is no clarity in either, or when there seems to be strong certainty in both, we must hold our positions with humility, wisdom, and grace, and await the time when the issues become more certain.

But on this we must agree: just as the biblical interpreter and preacher do much to expose the glories of God's written Word, so too does the scientist as he exposes the wonders of nature. Both reveal God's glory. God as the Creator makes the study of science an alluring calling for the Christian. The scientist reads the very fingerprints of God in the intricacy and beauty of the good creation. Creation's complexity speaks of God's intelligence and power. Creation's beauty

---

20 'The heavens declare the glory of God, and the sky above proclaims his handiwork' (Ps. 19:1).

speaks of His aesthetic sensibility. That it is winding down, and in many respects is dangerous to life, speaks deeply, and sadly, of the fall (of which we shall soon speak) which has darkened it.

There is wonder in creation that we will be forever uncovering, and, in uncovering some of that wonder, we discover something more of the greatness and of the glory of God.

7 THE WONDER OF HUMANITY

> Q. 10. How did God create man?
> A. God created man male and female, after his own image, in knowledge, righteousness and holiness, with dominion over the creatures.

'How do you make your chili?'

'Well, first I brown a pound of hamburger with some onions and green pepper, and then I…'

'No, that's not what I mean. What I mean is, what is the nature of the chili you make? Is it sweet or spicy or what?'

The second question is a different question than the first and is what the Catechism is asking here. It is not one of the process God used in creating humanity, but what the nature of that humanity is. And the answer comes to us in a series of affirmations.

First, man, defined interestingly and wonderfully as male and female, is a special creature. Humanity is the culmination of God's creative work. All else was created to provide the context in which Adam, the first man, and Eve, the first woman, and their descendants,[21] would live. Mankind is set apart from the rest of creatures and is wonderfully made 'a little lower than the angels.'[22]

This special creation of God is composed of two physical genders. Both, men and women, are equally created before God and equally share all that is said to be true of either as humans. Man, that is, male and female, bears the image of God. Such does not mean that we 'look like' God in a physical sense, but that in our capacity for knowledge and creativity, in our moral sensibility, and in our occupying a special place in the created order, we 'image' God. To look at any human is to see something of the nature of the God who created us.

This is not true just of white European males. It is not just true of those who can speak or walk or productively put in an eight-hour workday. This is true of all people, born and unborn, white or black, male or female, rich or poor, Christian or Muslim, nice or mean, free or imprisoned, fully abled or disabled, mentally stable or mentally ill. All the judgments we might bring to bear upon groups of people to divide them cannot separate them from the image of God they bear. The esteem with which we hold all others must be guided by this reality.

---

21 Throughout the Catechism the conviction is maintained that all humanity descended from this original pair. The genealogy of Jesus Himself is traced to this Adam (see Luke 3:23-38).

22 'Yet you have made him a little lower than the heavenly beings and crowned him with glory and honor' (Ps. 8:5).

As those created in God's image, we have dominion over the world in which we have been placed. We are stewards, ruling in God's place over creation. This commits us all to things like the ethical treatment of animals or to the proper care for rainforests and polar ice caps. We may differ with how we care for these things, but that we are to do so should never be questioned.

A part of exercising care over creation and reflecting the image of God is the human impulse to create. We are so formed that, like our Creator, we desire to make of the world something beautiful. This impulse is in some people suppressed and in others abused, but it is a part of our imaging of God. When a woman plants a garden in front of her South African hovel to beautify a patch of ground in an otherwise ugly place, she is expressing her irrepressible nature as one made in God's image. So, too, when an engineer cannot help but make the bridge aesthetically pleasing, or when the husband in charge of dinner folds the napkins and places a candle on the table to make it pretty, they image their Creator. You and I from our very nature are moved to create.

Such is how God created man. Since the original creation we bear that image poorly. We are like a mirror, cracked and caked with dirt, but no person ever loses his status as a bearer of the image of his Creator.

8 THE PROVIDENCE OF GOD

Q. 11. What are God's works of providence?
A. God's works of providence are his most holy,
wise, and powerful preserving and governing all his
creatures, and all their actions.

Brett was a bright, joyful child with leukodystrophy. When I met him he was confined to a wheelchair, knew that Jesus loved him, and did everything possible, fruitlessly as it turned out, to cheer on the Chicago Cubs. By age twelve his life had run its course. The level of grief involved in such a loss was captured for me in the anguish of another man who, having lost a child to disease, told me that we are never meant to outlive our children.

And yet many do, and those who have faced such sadness are sometimes prone to question the goodness and wisdom, if not the power or existence of God.

The Catechism, again echoing Scripture, presents God as personally, powerfully, and continually involved in His creation. He preserves all, not some, of His creatures, and governs all, not some, of their actions. This providence of God can be a great comfort. But when it crashes into the realities of natural disaster, devastating illness, and human evil, it leads to the agonizing but never answered cry of, 'Why?'

Such a question is proper. The biblical poets often raise such questions.[23] But to raise the question is to assume a god of providence. These questions make no sense if God did not have power and presence to affect the affairs of humanity. Indeed, the act of prayer itself makes little sense if there is not a god who engages with His world. It makes no sense to ask Him to move His hand toward a favorable outcome if such motion is off-limits or out of reach.

God has not relinquished or lost the power with which He created. He does not always answer our questions or satisfy our protests. He simply asks us to believe that His providence is not only powerful, but also holy and wise. It is this providence that led Jesus to the cross,[24] and it is this providence that raised Him from the dead. It is this providence that guarantees Jesus' return and the defeat of evil, and it is this providence that prepares a future for us with Jesus. It is this providence therefore that gives us our greatest hope.

The Apostle Peter invites us to place our worries before God because He cares for us.[25] Such care is not a mere generic sentiment but an active providence. By entrusting what we do not understand to God whom we know, we humbly acknowledge His power to deliver us from whatever

---

23 'How long, O LORD? Will you forget me forever?
   How long will you hide your face from me?' (Ps. 13:1).
   'O God, why do you cast us off forever?
   Why does your anger smoke against the sheep of your pasture?'(Ps. 74:1).

24 '… this Jesus, delivered up according to the definite plan and foreknowledge of God, you crucified and killed by the hands of lawless men' (Acts 2:23).

25 '…casting all your anxieties on him, because he cares for you' (1 Pet. 5:7).

we know not and consequently fear. Peter says: 'Humble yourselves, therefore, under the mighty hand of God so that at the proper time he may exalt you…'[26] assuming that the God of goodness and power will in fact raise us up and see us through the uncertainties of this world.

If He is powerful enough to preserve and govern even through what we do not understand, then He is powerful enough to preserve, protect, guide, and shepherd us to the ends we long for. I am willing to lay aside my lack of understanding for the comfort of knowing that when all is said and done, I am safe in His providential care.

After Brett died and the funeral was over I visited with his parents in their small, two bedroom house. The father made sure I saw a needlepoint artwork hanging on their wall. I'm not sure to whom the quote on it should be attributed, but it summarized this couple's understanding of providence—the truth that brought balm to their broken hearts.

> God is too good to be unkind and too wise to make mistakes.

So He is.

---

26 1 Peter 5:6.

3

The Brokenness of Creation

It is hard to hold on to an idea of God so grand as that which the Catechism has presented, when the idea of God itself in our day seems to have been shattered into a million pieces. In a famous twentieth-century study of American beliefs, Robert Bellah and his associates found that the religion favored by many was an individualistic set of beliefs centered around a belief in a god that fit their own notions of godness.[1] God was what we made Him to be. This has morphed, sociologist Christian Smith observed subsequently, into a current passion for what he calls 'moralistic therapeutic deism,' a generalized idea of a god that leads people to seek happiness and to be nice to one another.[2]

That people are forming ideas about God is a reflection that all were created to be in relationship with Him and bear His image. The fact that those ideas are so divergent and often wrong is a reflection that something disorienting and

---

[1] Robert Bellah, et al., *Habits of the Heart: Individualism and Commitment in American Life* (United States: University of California Press, 1996).

[2] Christian Smith, et al., *Soul Searching: The Religious and Spiritual Lives of American Teenagers* (United States: Oxford University Press, 2005).

degenerative has occurred to obscure the beauty of God's creation and to cloud human understanding of the Creator.

This disorienting and degenerative event known as 'the fall' is the source of all human misery and lostness. In a word, we who were created to be in relationship with the triune God are rebellious and broken.

But not beyond recovery and repair, as we will see.

9 THE COVENANT SET

> Q. 12. What special act of providence did God exercise toward man in the estate wherein he was created?
> A. When God had created man, he entered into a covenant of life with him, upon condition of perfect obedience; forbidding him to eat of the tree of the knowledge of good and evil, upon the pain of death.

Here the Catechism introduces the word 'covenant' as the way in which God has chosen to engage in a relationship with people. Covenant is an important idea which finds reflection in the many human relationships with which you are already engaged. You are related to parents and have friends. Perhaps you are married, perhaps you have children. Maybe you have siblings or have a job. All of these relationships come with guidelines governing them. Often these are unspoken and informal. Friendship, for example, comes with the expectation that one will keep secrets and be truthful and have each other's backs. These expectations and promises are no less real for not being written.

The rules governing other relationships are more formalized. It's a rule, for example, that employers treat their employees fairly and that employees give the effort they are paid to give. It is often wise that rules of this nature be written down in the form of a contract, a signed agreement binding the parties to uphold their end of the relationship.

You see, though the word 'covenant' may be unfamiliar to us, the idea is not. It is the way in which all relationships are guided and guarded. Covenants are binding commitments containing promises and obligations that are assumed by those who enter relationship with one another. Marriage, for example, is many things, but at heart it is a covenant between two people. The vows taken by a husband and a wife define a covenant between them, binding them to love, to guard, and to protect one another.

All these relationships reflect the way God enters into relationship with His created people. He enters into covenant with them.

In a covenant God binds Himself with promises and places obligations on those with whom the covenant is made. God manages His covenant relationship with His people through a representative person, through what is called a 'covenant head.' Those represented by the covenant head receive the promises and inherit the obligations of the covenant. It is much like when a president signs an alliance with a foreign government. The alliance is forged between the two heads of state, but the obligations and benefits of that alliance bind every citizen in both countries.

The initial covenant in the Bible is one made with Adam, and through Adam with all his descendants.[3] God's promise was one of life and continued delight in the paradise in which He had placed Adam. The only condition, the obligation placed upon Adam, was that he, and Eve with him, were free to eat any fruit from any tree in the garden with one exception. To Adam, and to us looking back through time, this restriction seemed arbitrary. And yet, it was a measure of Adam's covenantal commitment. Every covenant comes with promises and obligations. This was Adam's.

The results of this covenant will be addressed soon enough. Adam's failure necessitated a series of subsequent covenants with Noah and Abraham, with Moses and David, and ultimately with the head of a new covenant, Jesus.

The significant difference between ordinary covenants and the covenants of God is that those with whom God forms His covenant are not invited to participate. Rather, the covenant is imposed. This sounds oppressive, but it is really an act of God's kindness, His 'special act of providence.' In every case, the covenants were gracious movements of God toward His people. Never were or are they deserved, and never were or are their fruits earned. Through covenant God has sought and effected blessing for His people.

That God still chooses to govern His relationship with people through covenants should not surprise us. What should astound us is that He would choose to have a relationship with us at all.

---

3   '...descending from him by ordinary generation...', a distinction made by Q/A 16.

10 THE COVENANT BROKEN

Q. 13. Did our first parents continue in the estate wherein they were created?
A. Our first parents, being left to the freedom of their own will, fell from the estate wherein they were created, by sinning against God.

Q. 14. What is sin?
A. Sin is any want of conformity unto, or transgression of, the law of God.

Q. 15. What was the sin whereby our first parents fell from the estate wherein they were created?
A. The sin whereby our first parents fell from the estate wherein they were created was their eating the forbidden fruit.

The world closely examined makes us sad. Death and disease strike us personally and deeply. Systemic sorrows like poverty, oppression, and racism show how deep sadness can go. Many individual decisions and actions expose human brokenness and blindness. Each day reveals sadness and gives occasion to consider the nature of sin which, the Catechism will show, lies behind it all. All this is traceable to Adam and Eve, 'our first parents,' our covenant heads. They cared for creation and enjoyed unhindered blessing in fellowship with God, and then they turned.

The fall of Adam and Eve was precipitated by their eating the fruit they were not to eat.[4] Their act was a 'transgression of the law of God,' as the Catechism defines sin. But their act reveals a deeper issue. What lay beneath their choice was a determination to live independently of God. Yes, sin is observed, it is measured, it is defined by failure to keep God's commands, but in every sin there is the prior rejection of God. He is removed as our guide and replaced with something other. That is the heart of sin.

In the case of Adam and Eve, eating the fruit was the culmination of a series of considerations, which began with a determination that they understood reality better than their Creator. Satan, the enemy of good and of God, confused the couple regarding what God had actually commanded and then provoked them to question God's truthfullness and goodness. At that point, questioning what God had said, certain that He was more restrictive than necessary, and persuaded that God's threats and promises were empty, they ate.

If Adam and Eve had obediently walked away from the fruit, they would have by that action acknowledged that God is in fact good, that He is wise, and that His law is good. They would have shown that they understood that to flourish in the world given—that is, to find life—they would need to submit their free wills to His. This they did not do. And all too often we follow their lead.

---

4   These events are recorded in Genesis 3.

Yes, every sin is an act by which we fail to meet or actively defy God's command. But also, every sin is an act by which we supplant God with another, often ourselves with our own elevated judgment. This is what makes sin so…well … sinful. Eating a forbidden piece of fruit may not seem so bad. However, defying the holy God is. And by every sin we defy Him.

And the result is devastating. Every sin disrupts the 'shalom,' a Hebrew word often translated 'peace,' which speaks of the wholeness, the rightness, of the world that God has given. Sin is an attack on the beauty of God's perfection. Sin is contrary to the way things are supposed to be.[5]

Adam and Eve were moved by the freedom of their own will. We treasure that idea without thinking about its implications. In an orchestra, if the second trombone chooses to play every note a half step off from the score, in defiance of the conductor, because he treasures his freedom and will be the master of his fate and the captain of his soul,[6] then he may do so. But in so doing, he not only defies the conductor and makes himself subject to whatever judgment the conductor chooses to bring, he also attacks the beauty of the whole.

Sin is breaking God's law, certainly. But it is so much more, and so much uglier than we can ever imagine. It is the fountainhead of sadness.

---

5   An excellent book developing these points is *Not the Way Things Are Supposed to Be: A Breviary of Sin* by Cornelius Plantinga (United States: William B. Eerdmans Publishing Company, 1996).

6   From the poem 'Invictus' by William Earnest Henley.

11 Pervasive Guilt

> *Q. 16. Did all mankind fall in Adam's first transgression?*
> *A. The covenant being made with Adam, not only for*
> *himself, but for his posterity; all mankind, descending*
> *from him by ordinary generation, sinned in him, and fell*
> *with him, in his first transgression.*

Understandably, the subject raised by this Q/A is met with protests that it is unfair. There *is* something that seems grossly unfair about God's covenantal ways here. When God entered into a relationship with Adam, He did so through covenant. As such, the covenant was not just with Adam, but with his posterity so that all descending from him were 'in him,' that is, covenantally united with him.[7] That all seems fine to us until we realize that what it means is that when Adam, as our covenant head, sinned in the garden and fell under the judgment of God, *we* sinned and fell under the same judgment. Though we had yet to be born, when Adam fell we fell. Adam's guilt is our guilt. And that feels unfair.

When a whole classroom misses recess because Bobby or Janey talked out of turn, that *is* unfair for, in that case, the innocent suffer with the guilty. But covenant guilt is different. When Adam sinned, given that you and I were covenantally *in* Adam, then it is right and proper to say that when he sinned, we sinned. All that results from that sin rightfully falls on us not because the innocent are being

---

7   The Catechism's qualifier 'by ordinary generation' excludes Jesus, whose birth of a virgin was clearly extraordinary.

swept up with the guilty, but because we are, in fact, guilty. We 'sinned in him, and fell with him' and so we are guilty.

It feels unfair. Some recoil when realizing that this applies even to those who have yet to sin in the way Adam sinned. A child newly born does not know the law, and cannot consciously know that he transgresses the command of God. And yet, as he was in Adam when Adam sinned, this child sinned in Adam and fell with Adam and bears Adam's guilt as if it were his own, for it is his own. This is one of the implications of God dealing with us all through covenants.[8]

And yet, unfair though it seems by our standards, we should not wish it to be any other way. Certainly, were Adam not our covenantal head, we each still amass enough personal sin of our own commission to make Adam's sin look paltry. We clearly all stand under the judgment of God for our own sin. But the point of the idea we are considering here is that apart from all of that, in Adam there is sufficient guilt for our condemnation. We have sinned in ourselves and in Adam. We have cut ourselves off from all that is good and whole. What can be done?

What can be done, the Catechism will show us. The hint here is in the comfort the idea of covenant brings. What if God were to institute a new covenant with a new covenant head, one to stand in the place of Adam? What if this new covenant head were not to sin? What if this covenant head were to stand before God with pure righteousness? And what if this righteousness were to be credited[9] to those whom

---

8   These thoughts are developed in, among other places, Romans 5:12-21.

9   The theological word is 'imputed' which means 'to credit or ascribe (something) to a person or a cause'

He covenantally represented, as Adam's guilt was credited to those Adam represented? Is it in any way 'fair' that you or I should be counted righteous because someone else was righteous? Is this not unfair, that we should now be counted righteous because of another's righteousness?

This is not unfairness. This is mercy. And this is how the gospel of Jesus Christ comes to us.

12 PERVASIVE BROKENNESS

> Q. 17. Into what estate did the fall bring mankind?
> A. The fall brought mankind into an estate of sin and misery.

In Chaim Potok's wonderful novel, *My Name is Asher Lev*, the title character is a boy with a powerful gift of seeing and drawing the world. His dark drawings, however, are greatly disturbing to others in his Hasidic Jewish culture, and his mother urges him to draw pretty pictures. His response to her is sober: 'But it's not a pretty world.'[10]

Without question, there is beauty around us, but that beauty stands out precisely because of its contrast with the world's brokenness, the state of the world characterized by sin and misery. The next two sections will break this down in greater detail. For now, we must look at the reality that

---

https://www.merriam-webster.com/dictionary/imputed, accessed 12/10/19.

10   Chaim Potok, *My Name Is Asher Lev* (United States: Fawcett Crest, 1983), pp. 28, 29.

is around us and reckon with the fact that the brokenness and ugliness we see is the result of human transgression of a divine order.

Few question the world's brokenness. Wars and rumors of wars are not an end-of-the-world expectation but have been a reality ever since Cain took a club to Abel.[11] Love stories leading to wedding flowers and dancing warm our hearts, while those same hearts are broken by the necessity of domestic abuse shelters. Human achievements in technology, athletics, and art are celebrated while blind eyes are turned to the needs of the poor, the refugee, and the mentally ill. Children are murdered by madmen, innocents die in massive fires, tsunamis drown thousands, hurricanes strip the marginal of any hope. The planet warms, and politicians argue over its cause. Church leaders bicker, people leave one church for another, and pastors defile their high calling. No place, no time, no community, and no family is immune from sin and misery. It is not a pretty world.

The Catechism traces this state of affairs, all of it, to the fall, to the sin of our first parents, their decision on behalf of all their posterity to live life without God. Some shelve this explanation as no more than a quaint myth and offer their own. It was once thought that we would evolve beyond the observed depth of human evil. Two world wars have put that hope to bed for a time. Others suggest the cause for the world's misery lies in defects in brain chemistry that can be treated with the right medicine. Still others posit defects in human training to be overcome with better educational

---

11 'And when they were in the field, Cain rose up against his brother Abel and killed him' (Gen. 4:8).

methods and models. Some conclude that this is simply the way the world is and that it is beyond repair.

In the end no explanation for sin and misery has been given that is more plausible than the Christian one. God placed humanity in the role of caretakers of the world He created. Their unwillingness to honor Him in that role led to His judgment. 'You shall surely die,'[12] God had told them, and so death began to be a characteristic of the once perfect world. Earthquakes happen, viruses mutate, distrust and greed lead to wars, minds deteriorate, and people die, all because a judgment of death has been unleashed upon the world.

This human story, however long in its telling, does not and will not end with misery. The fall brought mankind into an estate out of which God in due time provides rescue. It is not a pretty world. But it is God's world. And this makes the Christian explanation of brokenness one that is full of hope.

13 PERVASIVE SINFULLNESS

Q. 18. Wherein consists the sinfullness of that estate whereinto man fell?
A. The sinfullness of that estate whereinto man fell consists in the guilt of Adam's first sin, the want of original righteousness, and the corruption of his whole nature, which is commonly called original sin; together with all actual transgressions which proceed from it.

---

12   Genesis 2:17.

People vigorously debate the fundamental nature of people. Some argue that people are basically good but flawed. Others believe that people are shaped toward evil or good by their environment. Still others discern a deep-seated propensity for evil within every person. Novelist Stephen King once observed: 'The potential lyncher is in almost all of us..., and every now and then, he has to be let loose to scream and roll around in the grass.'[13]

King as a careful observer of human behavior (as good novelists are) perceives by experience the point the Catechism makes theologically. Humanity is broken at its core. The fall has led to the full corruption of humanity's fundamental nature.

The Catechism reminds us of the point already made in our discussion of the covenant, that every human is guilty of Adam's first sin. We come into this world guilty and lacking in righteousness. But the point here goes further. We come into this world corrupt in every aspect of our being. We are touched in every point by the predisposition to self-serving independence and rebellion that characterized Adam's choice. As it has been put another way, we are by nature 'totally depraved.' We do not act out all the evil of which we are capable, but every part of us is turned inward and away from God. When we do what is judged to be good, that act is in contrast to our inherited nature, not symptomatic of it.

Human sinfullness is observed in our actual transgressions. It is felt when the hand slaps the face, it is heard when the racist remark escapes the lips, and it is seen when the rich

---

13 'Why We Crave Horror Movies', Stephen King, digital download-various sources; http://faculty.uml.edu/bmarshall/Lowell/whywe cravehorrormovies.pdf

man steers clear of the poor for fear of being compelled to part with his wealth. But these actions, these observable evils, proceed from our inherited natural tendency.

That people are not all monsters is due to God's restraining grace. God keeps the lyncher in most of us at bay. But that we are not monsters does not mean we are innocent. Ultimately we are guilty of Adam's first sin and our own, and each of us, monster or not, is desperately in need of rescue. Some of us are aware of that. The rest of us need to be.

14 Pervasive Sorrow

> Q. 19. What is the misery of that estate whereinto man fell?
> A. All mankind by their fall lost communion with God, are under his wrath and curse, and so made liable to all miseries in this life, to death itself, and to the pains of hell forever.

There was some great music on the US charts in May of 1966.[14] The Rolling Stones, The Mamas and the Papas, The Byrds, and Simon and Garfunkel hovered near the top of the lists. Further down and not so great, but still getting significant air play, was a sentimental song by Ray Coniff called 'Happiness Is….' The song made people feel good, but that good feeling strained against reality. In America,

---

14   According to, at least, me.

at least, it was not a happy time. Under the shadow of the Vietnam War, humanity was not reveling in happiness but in human misery that led some men to their deaths, that turned others into killers, and that encouraged some eventually to kill themselves.

The Catechism—not sentimental about the human condition—observes that in this life sadness often overwhelms happiness. The fall has brought an unshakeable misery upon the earth. What we should most greatly fear, the wrath and curse of God and the pains of eternal punishment, many of us only faintly grasp. What we directly confront are alienation and violence, exclusion and sickness, loss and hunger, injury and depression, and tears. We are indeed by the judgment of God made liable to all the miseries of this life.

We experience these miseries more intently because our hearts are created for something better. We long for happiness and wholeness. The Bible, we have mentioned before, encompasses this idea of wholeness with the Hebrew word 'shalom.' Cornelius Plantinga, whose book we have already mentioned, has helpfully defined shalom as '… universal flourishing, wholeness, and delight—a rich state of affairs in which natural needs are satisfied and natural gifts fruitfully employed, a state of affairs that inspires joyful wonder as its Creator and Savior opens doors and welcomes the creatures in whom he delights.'[15] Happiness is shalom, but shalom is the very thing that the fall undid. 'Shalom, in other words, is the way things are supposed to be.'[16] But clearly things are not the way they are supposed to be.

---

15   Plantinga, *Not the Way Things are Supposed to Be*, p. 10.
16   ibid.

The loss of shalom runs deeper than the miseries we observe. Though not something as tangible as the more visible miseries, at our core each of us longs for the communion we have lost with God. 'You have made us and drawn us to yourself, and our heart is unquiet until it rests in you,'[17] observed St Augustine many centuries ago, and he was right. Our hearts, apart from God, experience a perpetual state of dis-ease.

In the movie *Grand Canyon*, a man poised to be murdered and robbed by a gang of thugs is rescued by a tow-truck driver who observes about that situation and about life as a whole, 'Man, the world ain't supposed to work like this.'[18]

It's not, but for now it does. We suffocate under the hopelessness and realism of books and movies and art that tell us the unsentimental truth about life. And yet such truth leads us to long for what has been lost. We know there must be something more, something better. We long for happiness, for *shalom*. It is God's determination, in time, to provide it. To that end, He provides a redeemer.

---

17 Augustine of Hippo, *The Confessions*, tr. Maria Boulding (United States: New City Press, 1997), p. 39.

18 This also is referenced and developed by Plantinga in his insightful book.

4

The Provision of a Redeemer

When hiking along the Appalachian Trail in the Southeastern United States, one's heavy slogging is rewarded with occasional glimpses of great beauty. Then, in certain locations, the trail rises to follow the ridge. Here the hiker is given an uninterrupted and intoxicating view of remarkable beauty in every direction.

We have been slogging through some pretty heavy truths. While the sorrow and guilt and brokenness of humanity is important to be known, it presents an image of helplessness and lostness that can and often does lead to despair. Fortunately, the trail does not terminate there. In this chapter we ascend to a ridge from which we see Jesus. It is Jesus who will occupy our attention in this chapter.

To many, Jesus is merely the founder of a religion. There is some truth to that, of course. But as the Catechism here shows, He is far more than that. He is the Son of God and the redeemer of a fallen people. For that fallen people He is a gift of great beauty to be relished for eternity. We get to walk along this ridge for a while and capture a glimpse of that beauty.

15 GOD'S RESCUE

> *Q. 20. Did God leave all mankind to perish in the estate of sin and misery?*
> *A. God having, out of his mere good pleasure, from all eternity, elected some to everlasting life, did enter into a covenant of grace, to deliver them out of the estate of sin and misery, and to bring them into an estate of salvation by a redeemer.*

Had the question asked here, 'Did God leave all mankind to perish…' been answered with a simple 'yes,' the Catechism would never have needed to have been written. This infinite, eternal, and unchangeable God could have chosen to leave His creation to His creature's covenantal choice and abandoned the project as a lost cause. All mankind would have perished justly in the estate of sin and misery, and God would be no less righteous or noble for it. If He were then to be known at all, He would be known as one perfectly and fully just in all His ways. There could be none to bring any charge against Him. Humanity had made its choice.

But that is not what God chose to do. That He made a choice, that He chose to act in a way that would rescue people, that is, bring them 'into an estate of salvation,' is the primary act by which God should be understood. The fully just God, the one of absolute and perfect holiness, this God chose to act with mercy, to bring His people to a place that their actions did not deserve. He chose to rescue rebels out of the consequences of their rebellion into the place of His favor, and He chose to do so in spite of their determination to reject Him. In mercy He determined to retrieve them from their foolishness and to give them what they sought but could never find apart from His intervention.

I'm dancing around some words here that either mystify because of unfamiliarity or obscure the truth because of over familiarity. Words like 'covenant' (which we've already discussed), 'everlasting life,' 'elected,' 'salvation,' and 'redeemer' are wonderful words which we may or may not understand rightly. Some of them confuse us, and each could justify a lengthy consideration.

Perhaps the most puzzling and troubling word, the word most liable to upset our thinking about God is the simple word 'some.' The covenant with Adam was made on behalf of *all* humanity and so *all* fell when Adam fell. But God here enters into a covenant that is limited. He resolves to elect *some* but not all. To elect *some* to life is to abandon others to its opposite. This is unsettling. Yes, those whom God passes by are those who in Adam have already chosen their fate, but so had the some who are rescued.

This is unsettling largely because we cannot see with the eyes of God or know all that He intends. We are never meant to try to uncover God's ways. What we are meant to do is to ponder in amazement that, totally apart from our deserving, we are among that some.[1]

---

1   I understand that this insufficiently treats a subject that is a stumbling block to many. We are taught election in the Bible, it seems to me, so that we might know the depth of God's love for us, the reach of His compassion, and to be assured that those whom God chooses He cannot lose. Others, the identity of whom we are incapable of defining, we must leave to His wisdom and mercy.

What must not be obscured or lost is the central theme that God did not leave His people to die. A vast number, a 'some' that numbers more than the stars in the sky or sand on the seashore,[2] He did not leave to the consequences of their sin. He did not leave them to eternal misery but chose, rather, to deliver them, to rescue and to redeem them.

And why? Because of His mere good pleasure. Because it pleased Him to do so. It made Him happy to pursue us. It was His delight to rescue you.

And that is the most stunning reality of all.

16 JESUS – HIS NATURE

> Q. 21. Who is the redeemer of God's elect?
> A. The only redeemer of God's elect is the Lord Jesus Christ, who, being the eternal Son of God, became man, and so was, and continues to be, God and man in two distinct natures, and one person, forever.

There is a scene in the classic 1959 movie *Ben Hur* in which the enslaved hero of the movie, Judah Ben Hur, is driven parched and bitter with other slaves across the desert and past a figure we later learn to be Jesus of Nazareth. The face

---

2   Compare the promise to Abraham: 'I will surely multiply your offspring as the stars of heaven and as the sand that is on the seashore' (Gen. 22:17) with its fulfillment in heaven: 'I looked, and behold, a great multitude that no one could number, from every nation, from all tribes and peoples and languages, standing before the throne and before the Lamb' (Rev. 7:9).

of Jesus is never exposed to the camera. We see, however, a figure with unruffled, slightly wavy brown hair touching the collar of his robe moving slowly and gracefully to the side of Judah Ben Hur to offer him water.

The compassion of this scene is genuine. The physical image problematic. When Jesus' character is packaged in such a weak, otherworldly, nearly bodiless persona it becomes hard for modern people to see Jesus as the fully rounded person He was and as He is represented to us in the Bible.[3] The 'redeemer of God's elect,' as the Catechism has introduced Him, is a far more complex and unique character than our artists can convey.

Since God deals with His people covenantally, the redeemer who would be the head of a new covenant to rescue fallen humanity had to be human. Scripture presents Jesus as the fully human, adopted son of a carpenter named Joseph, miraculously conceived in the virgin womb of His mother, and Joseph's wife, Mary. He was born in the small town of Bethlehem, a descendant of Israel's great king David, and raised in the Galilean town of Nazareth. We can infer that as a child, being human, He got colds, skinned His knees, grew tired, and, contrary to the Christmas song,[4] cried when in need. He was a human child who grew up to be a human man. He was completely and fully human.

In His thirtieth year He gathered disciples and began to travel, to teach, and to do remarkable things, miraculous

---

3   Particularly in the Gospels, the first four books of the New Testament, Matthew, Mark, Luke, and John.

4   The carol 'Away in a Manger' has a line '… the little Lord Jesus, no crying he makes,' which reflects the tendency we have to isolate Jesus from His full and complete humanity.

things, which left ordinary people amazed and the authorities perplexed. His actions seemed to claim rights that belonged only to God. He forgave sin, He commanded storms, and He allowed men to bow before Him in worship. Some judged such things to be blasphemous because by them Jesus was acting like God.

His followers, however, slowly put the pieces together. Speaking for them all Peter declared that Jesus was the Son of God,[5] a radical confession which a later follower, Paul, explained as meaning that in Jesus '...the whole fullness of deity dwells bodily.'[6] This Jesus, completely and fully human, was also completely and fully God.

Being both God and man, Jesus possessed both a human and a divine nature. And yet He is one person. He is not divided or confused. He is not a 'Jesus Blend' like one might find among coffee beans. He does not possess two separate consciousnesses. There is never any internal argument raging in Him between His god nature and His human nature. When He prays, He is not talking to Himself. He is a singular person with two natures. We bow before this as a mystery, as something that we cannot fully comprehend but which is true.

We struggle to put it together, and yet the people who saw Him and lived with Him and heard Him did not respond to Him as a theological curiosity to be examined, dissected, and debated. He moved them by His teaching as no other, and in His eyes and actions they saw boundless compassion, courage, and wisdom. They saw Him as a person they wanted to follow, as should we.

---

5 'You are the Christ, the son of the living God' (Matt. 16:16).

6 Colossians 2:9.

After Jesus' death, two of His disciples, walking away from Jerusalem, were deep in conversation when a stranger (or so He first appeared) asked what they were talking about. In response, we read: 'And they stood still, looking sad.'[7] They were not sad because a theological oddity had been taken from them. They were sad because they had lost a friend who had loved them.

This is the redeemer of God's elect.

17 JESUS – HIS PERFECTION

Q. 22. How did Christ, being the Son of God, become man?
A. Christ, the Son of God, became man, by taking to himself a true body and a reasonable soul, being conceived by the power of the Holy Ghost in the womb of the virgin Mary, and born of her, yet without sin.

Q. 23. What offices does Christ execute as our redeemer?
A. Christ, as our redeemer, executes the offices of a prophet, of a priest, and of a king, both in his estate of humiliation and exaltation.

If you were to sit a fifteen-year-old Jesus down for a game of chess, would you have a chance of winning? Or, if basketball

---

7   Luke 24:17. The 'stranger' was Jesus whom they were at that point unable to recognize.

had been invented, would Jesus have ever missed a free throw? Would He have been able to draw like da Vinci and conceive of the universe like Einstein?

On the one hand those questions seem ludicrous. And yet answering them forces us to view the common idea of Jesus' perfection with some perspective. He was a man, and as a man He possessed a true and real body and a soul which reasoned and functioned humanly. His true body was not therefore athletically perfect. His reasonable soul would not necessarily see any more moves ahead on the chess board than you or I could. There is no reason to think that He knew more about relativity than I (which isn't saying much) and were He to have painted what He saw at the last supper, it may not have had the lasting power of da Vinci's later vision.

Jesus' perfection lay not in His abilities, which are the product of nature and nurture. His perfection lay rather in His sinlessness, an attribute unknown among other men. He was conceived without the stain of original sin. Throughout His life He was tempted in all those ways that people are tempted to sin. But these He consistently resisted.[8] He would not move a piece when His opponent was not looking. He would not claim to have built a table that in fact was the work of His father. He would have admitted that He fouled the shooter.

I don't think we need to assume therefore that He imagined killing Herod or fantasized about what He and Mary Magdalene might do after midnight. And yet in some manner He was tempted to sin, to set Himself above His Father and to stand against His Father's law, and in every case He chose faithful obedience to the Father.

---

8   'For we do not have a high priest who is unable to sympathize with our weaknesses, but one who in every respect has been tempted as we are, yet without sin' (Heb. 4:15).

Among the reasons why this is important is that His faithful obedience allowed Him to fulfill the roles which provided for our rescue. In Israel there were three offices—all of which bridged the space between God and His people—the prophet, the priest, and the king. In the past, these offices could only be filled by imperfect and sinful people. Jesus was sent and was able to fill them perfectly and sinlessly. By His faithful execution of these roles, He secured our rescue, our redemption.

For this He had no need for a perfect jump shot.

18 Jesus the Prophet

> Q. 24. How does Christ execute the office of a prophet?
> A. Christ executes the office of a prophet, in revealing to us, by his word and Spirit, the will of God for our salvation.

In popular vernacular a prophet is someone who has an uncanny ability to tell the future. In the Bible a prophet is one who has the divinely given ability to tell the truth. Sometimes this involved the future, of course. But truth was the prophet's focus, and the truth of the prophet in Israel was the truth given to him by God. The prophet spoke the truth of God to God's people. When Moses, a prophet of God, was nearing death, he spoke of another prophet whom

God would raise up,[9] one who like him would be close to God and as a prophet speak the truth of God. It is into this role, this office, that Jesus was placed. He was the prophet for whom Israel looked.

So fully did Jesus inhabit this office that the Apostle John tells us that He not only spoke the Word of God but that He *was* the Word. He tells us that when Jesus came, 'the Word became flesh and dwelt among us.'[10]

He fulfilled this office well. Some of His teaching was captured by the apostles and written down in the Gospels.[11] Those who heard Jesus speak noted the inherent authority in His words. He was not like other teachers, who linked the authority of their words to the authority of others who had come before them. Jesus spoke the truth of God and the authority of His words needed no further attestation.

Some Bibles are fond of printing what they call the 'words of Jesus' in red print. This recognizes the prophetic authority of Jesus' words which is good, but it is incomplete and potentially misleading. Jesus is the prophet behind all that is written in the New Testament. After Jesus' death He gave to the Church His Holy Spirit to continue to shape the words that were spoken and preserved concerning Him.[12] Luke, who wrote the gospel that bears his name

---

9   'The LORD your God will raise up for you a prophet like me from among you, from your brothers—it is to him you shall listen' (Deut. 18:15).

10   John 1:14.

11   John also tells us: 'Now there are also many other things that Jesus did. Were every one of them to be written, I suppose that the world itself could not contain the books that would be written' (John 21:25).

12   Of the Holy Spirit more will be said later.

as well as the Book of Acts, characterized the first book as the one where he recorded what 'Jesus began to do and teach.'[13] The Book of Acts contains what Jesus continued to do and teach through the apostles whom He called. A case could be made that if we highlighted the words of Jesus, then the entire New Testament (indeed, the whole Bible) would be red.[14]

The existence of a prophet's words, however, is not as remarkable as the content of those words. This prophet, Jesus, has come with a word from God to a lost people to show them the way home. He has come to reveal to those with ears to hear God's desire for their salvation. And the words He spoke, and the life He lived, showed that the will of God for the salvation of His people was not what they must do to find their way home, but what He was doing and now has done to bring them home. This is a much more gracious word than any could hope to hear.

A person lost in the desert will not draw much benefit from her fortune being told. On the other hand, if someone came and told her the true path to true water, that one would be celebrated.

Jesus is such a person, the prophet about whom God said: 'This is my beloved Son; listen to him.'[15]

---

13 Acts 1:1.

14 The New Testament is that portion of the Bible beginning with the book of Matthew and ending with the Book of Revelation.

15 Mark 9:7.

19 JESUS THE PRIEST

> *Q. 25. How does Christ execute the office of a priest?*
> *A. Christ executes the office of a priest, in his once*
> *offering up of himself a sacrifice to satisfy divine justice,*
> *and reconcile us to God; and in making continual*
> *intercession for us.*

In Terry Gilliam's 1991 movie, *The Fisher King*, Jack Lucas is a radio 'shock jock' whose careless on-air rantings lead a listener to commit a murder for which Lucas ultimately, and rightly, feels responsibility. An innocent woman died, and Jack cannot shake the weight of his culpability. Overwhelmed, he cries out to an empty room, 'I wish there was some way I could just pay the fine and go home!'

This is the deeply felt cry of everyone when finally made aware of their sin. Guilt is that inner anguish born from the sense that we have done wrong for which there needs to be some form of justice. Damage has been done and payment of some kind is due. Deep in our souls we know that our sin has separated us from a holy God and has merited His just anger and that there is nothing, ultimately, we can do to repair the damage. There is no place we can go to pay the fine, a fine we could not afford if there were.

That would leave us in despair had not God, in His covenantal kindness, opened a way for His people to be relieved of their guilt. In ancient Israel God provided this way through priests and the sacrifices they would offer.

Those sacrifices were, ordinarily, specially purified animals set apart for this special ceremony. These innocent creatures would be killed, sacrificed, because of the sinfullness of those who offered them. This ceremony provided a way for God's justice to be satisfied. The guilty would consider themselves united with the sacrifice so that when the sacrifice was complete, they could know they were forgiven. God had declared that He would look upon that sacrifice as sufficient so that the offerers could know that their guilt was removed and their sin atoned for. They could know forgiveness and could rest in a renewed relationship with God.

The priest who offered the sacrifice was the one provided by God, through whom the faithful could know that, despite their sin, they would be accepted by God. This all was a beautiful expression of the mercy of God. And yet, the fix was symbolic and temporary. Given the depth of human sin and the infinite purity of God, no priest was sufficiently pure to offer a fully effective sacrifice, and no sacrificial animal was sufficiently pure to be that sacrifice. And so the sacrifices had to be repeated time and time again. The cost of justice was that great.

Into this context Jesus, the perfect Son of God, came as a priest. Fulfilling this office He offered a single sacrifice to bear the sin of all God's people. The sacrifice that Jesus offered on our behalf was not a spotless sheep or perfect ox, but one perfect and undefiled and sufficient in purity to match the infinite stain of sin. Jesus as priest offered Himself as the sacrifice. In so doing, Jesus took upon Himself the divine justice sin deserved so that, united with Him in His sacrifice, sinners such as you and I are welcomed into the presence of God. He pays our fine that we might go home, and He stands forever as a reminder of our acceptance.

There had been many priests in Israel. They came and went and the offerings continued. In Jesus, once for all, in full perfection, the sacrifices came to an end. He was and is the great high priest whom all the other priests anticipated and in His sacrifice, all former sacrifices found their power.

As priest, Jesus paid our fine. Now we may go home. Forgiven. Forever.

20 Jesus the King

> Q. 26. How does Christ execute the office of a king?
> A. Christ executes the office of a king, in subduing us to himself, in ruling and defending us, and in restraining and conquering all his and our enemies.

Ask any child raised in a conservative Christian home what she knows about Jesus and she is likely to respond, 'He died on the cross for my sins.' That's understandable. We tend to emphasize Jesus' office of priest thinking mostly of our need for the forgiveness of sins.

And yet if that same child has been raised hearing C. S. Lewis' *The Chronicles of Narnia* read to her and we were to ask her who Aslan is, she is likely to inform us without hesitation that he is the lion, the king of Narnia.[16] It is to be lamented that Jesus' kingly role does not come as readily to

---

16 For those unfamiliar with these tales, we urge you to remedy that immediately! Aslan is the lion who represents Christ in the world of Narnia.

our minds as it does with Aslan. For Jesus is the king o̶ ....
world as Aslan is of Narnia.

But what does a king do? That kings rule we know,
but rule is more than mere command. The king rules by
protecting his subjects and, if they are captured, by rescuing
them. It is this fuller picture of the king that Jesus (and
Aslan, for that matter) fulfills.

This world that belongs to God is territory occupied
by a cruel and wicked usurper. Satan in ages past deceived
Adam and Eve and plunged our world into darkness. He
has subjected men and women ever since, blinding them to
the truth, keeping them in darkness, and binding them to
his service. Nevertheless, they are still God's people, and to
deliver them from this bondage God sent His son as king to
reclaim lost territory and to effect their rescue.[17]

As a king Jesus breaks the power of the usurper and opens
the way for our allegiance to be restored to the true and
rightful king. (All this will be unfolded in the chapters that
follow.) With our allegiance won and our bondage broken,
this king, Jesus, rules with benevolence and wisdom through
His Word and Spirit. (All this too will concern us in later
chapters.)

The King's enemy does not let go of lost rule lightly.
Having had his dominion stripped, he sees God's people as
prey to devour, and he exercises every bit of subtlety to win
them back and if possible to destroy them. Satan hates God
and labors to defame and defile those who follow Him. He
spares no effort to undermine Christian allegiance, whether

---

17 'He has delivered us from the domain of darkness and transferred us
to the kingdom of his beloved Son, in whom we have redemption,
the forgiveness of sins.' (Col. 1:13-4)

through active persecution, physical or mental trauma, or deceit and trickery. Right and left Christians are tempted to abandon their commitment to the new and rightful King. But this King not only rules us. He defends us.

Since this rightful King is good and powerful, Christians need not fear. He defends us with vigilance and will not be defeated. Yes our enemies, both visible and invisible, loom large. These He restrains now and will in time fully conquer. He holds us in the palm of His hand and no power on earth or of hell can dislodge us. Those the King rescues He secures. He who rules and defends us and restrains even now our enemies, will, certainly and without question, conquer them all. Which in the end is the story of Aslan and Narnia. Aslan, who set Narnians free, set them free to enjoy the delight of His rule into eternity. In this way we celebrate Jesus as our rightful and faithful King.

21 JESUS HUMILIATED

> Q. 27. Wherein did Christ's humiliation consist?
> A. Christ's humiliation consisted in his being born, and that in a low condition, made under the law, undergoing the miseries of this life, the wrath of God, and the cursed death of the cross; in being buried, and continuing under the power of death for a time.

For Jesus, life was sacrifice. He was the Son of God born into a poor family in a marginalized community. He was a king subject to hunger and weariness and all other experiences of human deprivation. He never sinned, and yet He died bearing a curse from which He was by nature exempt. For Jesus, life was sacrifice that plunged Him into the depths of humiliation. Many others, of course, suffer and are brought low. And yet we have reason to claim that no person ever traveled such a distance in his humiliation as Jesus.

In thinking about Jesus' humiliation we are rightfully brought to thoughts of His death. To think about His death is to consider the brutal agony that was Roman crucifixion. I cringe merely at the thought of nails driven through flesh, but that was just the beginning. Those crucified did not die from that pain or the resulting loss of blood but from asphyxiation. Being suspended from hands and feet creates a situation where breath comes only by pulling oneself up, straining the muscles and tearing at the nail-pierced hands. Eventually the pain required to breathe becomes so great, and the body so weak, that the crucified man can no longer endure the effort. Gasping for air he dies. This can take many hours and often took days. That Jesus died in only six hours surprised those accustomed to crucifixions.

Jesus' death was brutal, but it was no more brutal than the equally tortuous deaths which many others throughout history have faced, sometimes with outstanding courage and tranquility. Certainly it is worth noting that Jesus was uniquely the Son of God, the Creator of all, the giver of life. It was incongruous that one such as He should die, be buried, and be confined to a tomb. But something else was at play on the cross that made Jesus' death uniquely terrible. It is that He, the Son of God, there experienced His Father's wrath. This envelops the cross with a solemnity that cannot be ignored and separates it from every other human experience of death.

There was a depth of anguish in His cry: 'My God, why have you forsaken me?'[18], that can only allude to the great abyss into which this humiliation had plunged Him. He who was the Word of God, He who had for eternity looked into the face of His Father and seen only love, then heard only silence and could see no loving face. He who is forever one with His Father sensed only alienation. This is the heart of His agony, and it is the focal point of His suffering. Into this the human mind is ultimately unable to peer. Theologian John Murray's words invite pause and wonder:

> Here we are the spectators of a wonder the praise and glory of which eternity will not exhaust. It is the Lord of glory, the Son of God incarnate, the God-man, drinking the cup given him by the eternal Father, the cup of woe and of indescribable agony. We almost hesitate to say so. But it must be said. It is God in our nature forsaken of God…. There is no reproduction or parallel in the experience of archangels or of the greatest saints. The faintest parallel would crush the holiest of men and the mightiest of the angelic host.[19]

This is the suffering of Jesus. This is the pinnacle of His life of sacrifice. This is the depth of humiliation He was willing to endure. And remarkably we are told that He endured this

---

18 'And at the ninth hour Jesus cried with a loud voice, "Eloi, Eloi, lema sabachthani?" which means, "My God, my God, why have you forsaken me?"' (Mark 15:34).

19 John Murray, *Redemption—Accomplished and Applied* (United States: William B. Eerdmans Publishing Company, 1955), pp. 90-1.

for 'the joy set before him.'[20] What joy could there be that would lead Him to travel to such terrible depths? It was the joy of our rescue.

> *Amazing love! How can it be*
> *that thou, my God, shouldst die for me?*[21]

22 JESUS EXALTED

> Q. 28. Wherein consists Christ's exaltation?
> A. Christ's exaltation consists in his rising again from the dead on the third day, in ascending up into heaven, in sitting at the right hand of God the Father, and in coming to judge the world at the last day.

> *'Christ is risen!*
> *He is risen indeed!'*

This proclamation, spoken literally within some traditions of Christianity but in essence in them all, is not only the central affirmation of our Christian faith, it is also the most stabilizing. For if there is one thing that is true of all Christians, whether they confess it or not, it is that we all confront occasional bouts of doubt. And if there is one

---

20 '[Jesus]…who for the joy that was set before him endured the cross, despising the shame, and is seated at the right hand of the throne of God' (Heb. 12:2).

21 Charles Wesley, 'And Can It Be?' *The Trinity Hymnal, Revised Edition* (United States: Great Commission Publications, 1990), #455.

reality that has the power to put those doubts to rest, it is the exaltation of Jesus, particularly His bodily resurrection.

Many things stir up doubts in Christians. Some are pushed to doubt by suffering and others by intellectual curiosity. Some are hurt by the church and others simply grow disinterested. Missionary theologian Francis Schaefer was shaken to his core by 'the lack of love shown between Christians.'[22] Philosopher Nicholas Wolterstorff struggled with doubt after the death of his twenty-five-year-old son Eric.[23] Doubt propelled both men to a reconsideration of the resurrection, and there they found stability.

It is possible that doubt has driven you to read a book on the Catechism. Perhaps there are doubts lingering in your heart from personal pain or struggle. Perhaps you are stung by the doubts of others. Doubts may not go away easily, but they are critically weakened when confronted with the truths surrounding the resurrection of Jesus.

When Christians recite, 'The third day he rose again from the dead,'[24] they affirm the most momentous event in human history.[25] He who certainly died rose never to die again. Forty days after He rose, He ascended visibly into the heavens. There, as He had foretold, He has been installed

---

22 Francis Schaefer, *True Spirituality*, introduction by Jerram Barrs (United States: Tyndale House Publishers, 2001), p. xvi.

23 Nicholas Wolterstorff, *Lament for a Son* (United States: William B. Eerdmans Publishing Company, 1987).

24 The Apostles' Creed.

25 Jesus' resurrection is recorded in all four Gospels, in Matthew 28:1-15, Mark 16:1-8, Luke 24:1-12, and John 20:1-18. His ascension and exaltation is touched upon in some of these passages, along with Acts 1:1-11 and Philippians 2:9-11. The logic and theological implications of the resurrection are given thorough treatment by Paul in 1 Corinthians 15.

at the right hand of the Father to rule in glory. And as He promised, He will return to exercise a final act of judgment and of deliverance.

All this we affirm in the Catechism. That it happened in history is hard to deny.[26] That Jesus died and that His dead body was placed in a sealed tomb and that contrary to all expectation and all physical possibility, on the third day this same Jesus emerged from that tomb, leaving behind only the cloths used to wrap Him, is the historical boundary marker between Christianity and every other religion. His resurrection vindicated His humiliation and His suffering and led Him to His rightful place of rule as King at the right hand of the Father.

I have seen Christians hurt by the church. I know the struggle of suffering that leads to questions of the existence and care of God. I have watched as men and women are lured away from Christianity by other ideologies. But what I and others cannot escape is that something significant happened that third day. The tomb was vacated. Jesus, who died with love on His lips, rose with power in His hands, and He did so that those who are His would know life everlasting. We

---

26 Many, many competent, and compelling books have been written to answer those who protest the resurrection and to persuade those who are uncertain. Perhaps you have looked at these and found them unconvincing. I understand that, but I also think there is something in the perspective of the French Philosopher Blaise Pascal when he noted that in persuading someone of some aspect of religion we must '...make good men wish it were true, and then show that it is' (Penses, 12). If in sketching this whole picture of Christianity you might be moved to wish it were true, being in such a place does not change the evidence. It merely helps you see it with less resistance.

can struggle with much, but we cannot walk away from the resurrected Jesus.

Theologian Fleming Rutledge has written, perhaps with some allowable exaggeration, 'Many believers have a crisis of faith every few days.'[27] Timothy Keller has noted that 'A faith without some doubts is like a human body without any antibodies in it.'[28] You are not alone if you struggle with doubt. By all means wrestle with it and confront it. What you face is normal and has been faced and dealt with by others before you. And they have found, in the end, the stabilizing power of the resurrection.

> *[Jesus'] cross dispels each doubt; I bury in his tomb*
> *each thought of unbelief and fear,*
> *each ling'ring shade of gloom.*[29]

And so, we continue to affirm, with gratitude, joy, and relief,

> *Christ is risen.*
> *He is risen indeed.*

---

27 Fleming Rutledge, *The Crucifixion: Understanding the Death of Jesus Christ* (United States: William B. Eerdmans Publishing Company, 2017), p. 30.

28 Tim Keller, *The Reason for God* (United States: Dutton, 2008), p. xvi.

29 Horatius Bonar, 'Not What My Hands Have Done', *The Trinity Hymnal, Revised Edition*, #461, verse 4.

5

The Blessings of the Redeemed

In Dr Seuss's *Green Eggs and Ham*[1] the hero is so relentlessly pursued by Sam-I-Am that finally, worn down, and for no other reason than to get some relief, he consents to taste the offered green eggs and ham. Immediately his face fills with wonder, and he is transformed from one fleeing pursuit to one lost in love.

This analogy is apt here. The psalm invites us to '…taste and see that the LORD is good!'[2] In the sections that follow, this is what the Catechism does. It invites us so to taste and behold the astonishing good gifts of God that our faces might fill with wonder, and that we who were resistant in being pursued might be drawn to love our pursuer.

These sections reveal how recalcitrant sinners are brought from darkness to light, are transformed from rebel to child, and are renewed from lostness to holiness. Savor this! If you are not a Christian, may the wonder of this wear away your resistance. And if you are a Christian, may it lead you

---

1   Dr (Theodor Geisel) Seuss, *Green Eggs and Ham* (United States: Beginner Books, 1960).

2   Psalm 34:8.

to consider how greatly you are loved. You are the beloved child of God. This is the wonder of the gospel.

23 THOSE SOUGHT

> Q. 29. How are we made partakers of the redemption purchased by Christ?
> A. We are made partakers of the redemption purchased by Christ, by the effectual application of it to us by his Holy Spirit.

One dark, early morning my wife, Barb, called me from my daughter Adria's house and frantically asked for prayer. Adria had just given birth and her newborn son was not breathing. The midwife was calmly addressing the crisis, but Barb's anxiety had become fear. We hung up and I prayed.

Soon the phone rang again. 'He's okay!' Barb blurted out. This was the good news I had wanted to hear.

Christianity, too, is good news. That is how the Bible speaks of the life, death, and resurrection of Jesus Christ. It is the news people want to hear. Other religions and philosophies will, like Christianity, posit an ultimate purpose for life and offer standards of ethical behavior. Christianity is more than that. It is the intervention of God in history to do things through Jesus. Christianity is the announcement, the heralding, of these things. When the early Christians spoke about Christianity, they spoke about Jesus and called it 'good news.'[3]

But is it 'news' to us as the word of my grandson's recovery was news to me? Often, I fear, it feels to us more like mere history than current news. These events are interesting, but they happened all so long ago, and they feel disconnected from modern personal experience. To hear that my grandson was okay was news that for me was personally consequential, but to others it would have been merely interesting. The accounts of Jesus living, dying, and being raised strike some people as being at most interesting but in the end personally inconsequential. It is hardly good news.

So how are these things received as life-transforming good news? The answer which the Catechism gives and which it will begin to unpack in the next series of questions is that God enables His elect to see it as good news. God enables those for whom Jesus died and rose again to see that these things are in fact personally consequential. The initiative here is with God. He awakens Christians to the benefits secured by the redeemer as He applies those benefits to them. God acts particularly and He acts first.

That God acts particularly among the elect will continue to seem unsettling to some readers. I encourage you to reconsider the discussion of the nature of God in previous sections.[4] That He has sought you, Christian, is in fact a

---

3   To give just one example: 'Then Philip opened his mouth, and beginning with this Scripture he told him the good news about Jesus' (Acts 8:35).

4   Particularly worth re-visiting are the sections 'What God Does' and 'God's Rescue.'

deeply significant aspect of the good news which we ought not let slip by.

That God acts first seems counterintuitive and therefore puzzling in its own right. This is not the way most of us experience Christianity. Our experience is ordinarily one in which the initiative seems to be ours. *We* seek peace and find it in Jesus. *We* long for forgiveness and find it at the cross. *We* hear the good news and *we* respond to it in some way. It feels to us as if we are the ones moving toward God, not Him toward us. Is this wrong? Not at all.

We are the ones seeing and hearing and responding. That is our experience. But what lies behind our experience is the wonderful and gracious initiative of God. As an anonymous hymn writer once put it:

> *I sought the Lord, and afterward I knew*
> *he moved my soul to seek him, seeking me*
> *it was not I that found, O Savior true;*
> *no, I was found of thee.*[5]

Christians are Christians because God seeks, finds, and announces His good news to those whom He has chosen. The Christian is moved by this because God has moved our heart to seek Him. God makes this news consequential to us.

When I heard that my grandson was living and would bear my middle name, I wept with relief and joy. That news mattered to me. This news of Jesus matters in an even more fundamental and dramatic way (which the Catechism will help us explore).

And Christian, this is your good news.

---

5 *The Trinity Hymnal, Revised Edition*, #466.

24 THOSE IN UNION

> Q. 30. How does the Spirit apply to us the redemption
> purchased by Christ?
> A. The Spirit applies to us the redemption purchased by
> Christ, by working faith in us, and thereby uniting us to
> Christ in our effectual calling.

Last night I made a trip to the grocery store. I picked out
a bunch of bananas, and I paid the clerk the money she
said I owed for the bananas. It made sense. That's how the
marketplace works.

This is the way that many think Christianity works as
well. We set our sights on certain benefits and determine
to pay the necessary price to get them. We decide we
would like the happiness and friendship Christianity offers
and so to get that we commit to being faithful in church
attendance. We clean up our behavior and try to be nicer
to others. We begin to pray some and to read the Bible. It
works for bananas. But this is not how Christianity works.
'Marketplace Christianity' like this creates a very busy and
exhausting life which is at odds with the rest and joy of
which Jesus spoke.[6]

Christians receive the benefits of Christianity not through
what they pay nor through what they do, but through their

---

6   'Come to me, all who labor and are heavy laden, and I will give you
    rest. Take my yoke upon you, and learn from me, for I am gentle
    and lowly in heart, and you will find rest for your souls. For my
    yoke is easy, and my burden is light' (Matt. 11:28-30).

relationship, their covenantal union, with Christ.[7] By faith, Christians are united with Jesus. In union, all that is His becomes ours and all that is said to be true about Him is to be accepted as true about us.[8] 'In Him' (the common biblical phrase pointing to union), we have died. As He has been raised to life, so too, Christians, in Him, have been raised to life. As He is seated at the right hand of the throne of God, in Him, Christians are there too. In Him, we have forgiveness of sins and have been sealed by the Holy Spirit to receive an inheritance. We have never kept the law perfectly, and yet in Him, that is, through our union with Christ, we are considered to have done so. In Christ, in union with Him, we are judged righteous.

To believe in Jesus means far more than to accept a certain set of propositions as true, and to be a Christian means far more than living a certain kind of life. Christians are those united to Christ in all that He has done and accomplished. All the benefits of redemption come to us through this union. We walk out with all the 'goods' of redemption having paid nothing for them. What would get us arrested in the marketplace gets us life in Christianity.

There was a time I walked into a coffee shop and left without paying. A few months ago I placed my order at a local Starbucks and no money changed hands. I picked up my coffee and sat with Barb to enjoy it. I received all the benefits and paid nothing for them and no one stopped me at the door to read me my rights before hustling me off to jail.

---

7   We spoke of the covenant in the section 'The Covenant Set.'

8   Though developed in many places in the New Testament, this idea is seen clearly in Ephesians 1 and 2, from which many of the assertions in this paragraph are drawn.

This was not because I had an unspent credit or because I charmed the clerk into waving me on. Rather, it was a 'family and friends' opening of a new cafe. My son, Seth, was one of the baristas in that store. My drink came solely through my relationship with him. All the benefits of that store were mine because of my union with my son. I had access to what he had access to.

Of course, I can afford bananas and the occasional latte. But redemption? The cost of that was the death of the Son of God. I fool myself if I think I can pay a market price of good works and words for that. I can only come into this through union with Jesus, through whom I get far more than a free latte or a bunch of bananas.

25 THOSE CALLED

Q. 31. What is effectual calling?
A. Effectual calling is the work of God's Spirit, whereby, convincing us of our sin and misery, enlightening our minds in the knowledge of Christ, and renewing our wills, he does persuade and enable us to embrace Jesus Christ, freely offered to us in the gospel.

In Patrick O'Brian's novel, *The Far Side of the World*, Jack Aubrey is the captain of a ship in the British Navy during the days of the war of 1812.[9] Sailing an isolated expanse of

---

9   Patrick O'Brian, *The Far Side of the World* (United States: W. W. Norton, 1992).

the Pacific Ocean, the never sure-footed Stephen Maturin, Jack's good friend and the ship's surgeon, tumbles overboard. Confident that he could save his friend, Jack leaps in after him. But the ship sails on unaware that its captain and surgeon are floundering in its wake and desperately in need of rescue.

This pretty well pictures the state of humanity apart from God: floundering, in need of rescue, and, unlike Jack and Stephen, unaware of their danger. Humanity is not only lost, but under the active judgment of God. Though some might imagine ways of self-rescue,[10] those ways are as unrealistic as would be the prospect of Jack and Stephen swimming in some random direction hoping to find land in the middle of the Pacific. What humanity needs is what Jack and Stephen needed: to be sought and rescued. We have spoken about the steps that God has taken to make our rescue possible. In what is here called 'effectual calling' we consider the steps God takes to enable us to receive that rescue.

For this, God must first convince sinners that they need rescue.[11] Such convincing, though necessary, is nevertheless resisted. It is necessary because none will seek rescue if they have no awareness of their need to be rescued. It is resisted because people picture themselves the masters of their own fate and are loathe to admit need. To overcome this resistance God must convince us that we are sinful and miserable. Such persuasion may mean that we need to fail at

---

10 Peruse, for evidence, the 'self-help' or 'religion' sections of your local bookstore.

11 '…convincing us of our sin and misery…' is language meant to remind us of Q/A 17, addressed in the section 'Pervasive Brokenness.'

something or pass through a period of suffering. Something painful may be required because only by such can we be enabled to understand our true need, that we are alone at sea, and that our money or accomplishments or perfect life will not bring us the happiness we seek. Becoming a Christian always begins with God through the Holy Spirit convincing sinners of their need. Such is an act of tough love.

Sensing a need and finding a solution are different things, of course. And so the work of God's Spirit in effectual calling also involves 'enlightening our minds in the knowledge of Christ.' There are things we must know about the existence of God and the life and death of Jesus. We must be moved by His call for sinners to repent and be struck by the wonder of His resurrection. We may hear about these things through friends or through preachers, but it is the Holy Spirit who gives us understanding, who enlightens our minds to their truth.

Still to be overcome is the human impulse to fight battles alone and to rescue himself. God must give to the one effectually called a new heart. He '…[renews] our wills…' so that we might be both persuaded and enabled to accept the rescue offered by Christ. Such a renewal of the will, the giving of a new heart, is so fundamentally transforming that it is compared, in the language of the Gospel of John, to being born again.[12] Yes, the Christian chooses Christ as He is offered in the gospel. Yes, we embrace Him as a very real act of our will. But to do this, God must first soften our

---

12 'Jesus answered him, "Truly, truly, I say to you, unless one is born again he cannot see the kingdom of God"' (John 3:3).

stony and stubborn hearts, transforming them into those that are desperate for Him.[13]

At a deep and profound level, effectual calling is the greatest miracle any of us will ever experience. By His Spirit God removes all barriers and saves us from sin and misery. When we are helpless and without hope, He comes to us and rescues us.

When Jack and Stephen are eventually found and rescued by their shipmates, they are profoundly grateful. They are moved to see, as we are to see, that apart from the work of another, they would never have found rescue.

26 THOSE BLESSED

> Q. 32. What benefits do they that are effectually called partake of in this life?
> A. They that are effectually called do in this life partake of justification, adoption and sanctification, and the several benefits which in this life do either accompany or flow from them.

If you happen to come across a crying infant, giving him four tickets to Disney World and a voucher for airfare and lodging is not likely to make the crying go away. We have misread the child's need. God does not commit that mistake. As our Creator He knows what our hearts most desire and what our souls cry out for. And He gives it in our redemption.

---

13 This imagery is taken from Ezekiel 36:25-7.

French philosopher Luc Ferry believes that the fundamental human concern is how we make sense of life in the presence of the inevitability of death. That is, 'Is there a way to rise above death, to transcend it, to make sense of it, even to live a meaningful life in spite of it?'[14] Ferry is not a Christian and he discounts the Christian answers to his question. But as he surveys philosophy over the centuries he concludes that what we need as humans for happiness, what we are crying out for, is '...to be understood, to be loved, not to be alone, not to be separated from our loved ones—in short, not to die and not to have them die on us.'[15] Tickets to Disney World only mask that ache.

Death's impact upon life is in more than its terminal character. It overlays human experience with heartache and isolation and loneliness. Christianity is bold in its claim to offer life, to counter the terrible realities of death.[16] Through our union with Christ, the Catechism points out, we are justified, adopted, and sanctified. Though we have yet to define these terms, they reveal that Christianity addresses in a striking and audacious way the deep human desire for real happiness. In short, Christianity touches upon the deepest cries of your heart.

People are so desperate to know that they are loved, that they are accepted and that they are okay, that they exhaust themselves trying to earn it. They labor to make a name for themselves, to earn people's praise, to rise above shame, or to secure parents' approval. Such effort is not only fruitless but

---

14 Luc Ferry, *A Brief History of Thought: A Philosophical Guide to Living* (United States: Harper Perennial, 2011), p. 4.

15 ibid.

16 'I came that they may have life and have it abundantly' (John 10:10).

for the Christian, unnecessary. In justification, God declares that we are okay and that we are loved. Justification assures our weary souls that, in spite of all our missteps and failings, we are accepted.

But that is not all. Though life can feel like a lonely walk terminated by an empty eternity, such isolation is unnecessary. God adopts us into a family. God, who knows our faults and loves us still, welcomes us to a family from which we will never be cut off. He gives us a place, a home, and the rich privileges of being a child of God. We have a place.

And we want to flourish. We want not only to live, but we long to live wisely and joyfully. Christians are not left without direction or ability. God accepts, adopts, and then shapes His people into the way of life. He gives the direction for life as well as the motive and power to live.

In short, what the human heart longs to experience, Christianity provides. It is life that Christianity gives, and Christians gladly embrace this life even if it means, for some, a martyr's death. This sounds so counter-intuitive that some imagine that the benefits of Christianity are only received after death. That is not the case at all. Certainly these benefits are fully developed and experienced in eternity, but this life, eternal and abundant, is not something merely future. It is a future life whose impact permeates the life we live now.

We may not express the deep need of our soul in the terms the Catechism uses or even in the terms of classical philosophy. We may feel as aimless and confused as an infant wailing. But our God knows our need and meets it in ways that are rich beyond the greatest reaches of our imaginations. Disney tickets won't cut it. God gives us life in the face of death and that alone quiets our cries.

27 THOSE JUSTIFIED

> *Q. 33. What is justification?*
> *A. Justification is an act of God's free grace, wherein he pardons all our sins, and accepts us as righteous in his sight, only for the righteousness of Christ imputed to us, and received by faith alone.*

Cartoon images of heaven often feature a person standing on a cloud before a large desk behind which a haloed and bearded man guards admittance to eternal bliss. Before the bearded man sits a book and the jokes (and the tension) play on what the person might or might not have done and whether he will or will not get in.

These things are funny partly because they touch upon a deeper tension felt in different ways by everyone. Many struggle with a deep uncertainty as to whether they are 'okay' or good enough. Heaven may not be what we contemplate at a conscious level. Nevertheless we are concerned with being good enough to avoid exclusion from acceptance at some level. For the one who is aware of God this can become a fear that the good they have done is insufficient to gain acceptance before Him. Others are so aware of the failure in their lives that they believe themselves certain to be excluded from whatever heaven there might be.

This tension can reveal something true and something remarkable. First, it is true that we have not done sufficient good. It is true that our failure is disqualifying. But the remarkable thing is that these things, in the end, are not what determines our 'getting in.' God has freely given us ('an act of God's free grace') what we need.

When a Christian places his faith in Christ, a transaction occurs. In union with Him, the guilt for our insufficient works and our sinful acts is taken up by Jesus. This guilt becomes the guilt for which He endured death. That is the first part of the transaction. At the same time, Jesus' perfect record of obedience and goodness ('the righteousness of Christ') becomes ours[17], and on the basis of *His* record, now ours, we are justified. We are declared not only innocent, but fully righteous *in Him*.[18]

These questions still unsettle us: 'What if I mess it up? What if after being justified I sin and do really bad stuff? Would that not keep me out of heaven? Would that not disqualify me? Would not I then forfeit my acceptance?' A certain inbred (but erroneous) logic says that they would.[19] Covenantal logic says that they would not. Our acceptance before God rests on the work of Jesus, our covenant head, with whom by faith we are united. The Christian is declared righteous by God on the basis of Christ's righteousness, not his own. If in fact Jesus bore my guilt on the cross, then my guilt cannot lessen the power of that. It is ludicrous, really,

---

17   It is 'imputed,' that is, credited to our account, as our guilt is credited to His.

18   This is the fruit of God's covenantal relationship with His people, as we discussed in Q/A 16.

19   The logic of the marketplace, which we considered in Q/A 30.

to think that my sin would lessen the power of the death of Jesus.

In the same way, it is ludicrous to think that my righteousness adds anything to the record of Christ. I've been in a church since childhood. I briefly considered a missionary career, and I am now a pastor. But these things no more qualify me for God's favor than the acts and deeds of any other. At the same time, I have failed my wife, my children, and my God with acts and thoughts unworthy of my high calling as a Christian. And yet *these* things neither enhance nor detract from my acceptance before God. Our resumés are not relevant. It is only the resumé of Jesus that matters for our justification. Christians are secure, justified by a free gift of God, an act linked to Christ's righteousness alone.

Perhaps the cartoon imagery has some merit. We are before a desk, a judge's bench. Our whole life is laid out for inspection, written in the book before the judge. After carefully comparing this record of our works with the perfect law of God, the judge lifts his eyes to us, the defendant, and shocks us saying, 'Not guilty.' This stuns us because we know what we have done. Surely there must be some mistake. And so we ask to look at the book to make sure the judge is looking at the right pages. He is. What is written there on our pages is the perfect work of Jesus Christ. The verdict stands because of what the judge sees. He sees the perfect righteousness of Christ as ours. And so we stand before Him 'not guilty' and therefore welcome.

The cartoon images may or may not be funny. But this? It should make us laugh with joy, that such a remarkable thing could be true.

28 THOSE ADOPTED

> Q. 34. What is adoption?
> A. Adoption is an act of God's free grace, whereby we are received into the number, and have a right to all the privileges of, the sons of God.

I was not present for the birth of three of our six children. More surprisingly, neither was Barb, their mother. Their birth certificates record us as father and mother, but we were elsewhere those particular days. And yet these three are completely and fully our children. The fact that they came into our family through adoption makes no difference in their status. They have been subject to the same care and discipline (or lack!) that the others received. All six share equally in our love. Fully they are ours.

The Bible speaks of those who are united to Christ as having been not only justified but also adopted by God. This conveys the extent and depth of God's relationship with His people. We are His adopted children and He is our Father.

This *language* of adoption appears specifically in the Bible in several places[20], but the *idea* is throughout. Jesus particularly insisted that we see God as our Father. He taught us to pray to 'Our Father....'[21] He revealed that God as a

---

20 In the letters to the Romans and to the Galatians particularly.

21 'Pray then like this: "Our Father in heaven, hallowed be your name..."' (Matt. 6:9).

father loves to give good gifts to us, His children.[22] He noted that God's fatherly care for us is as tender and as detailed as that with which God cares for the birds.[23] Jesus' Sermon on the Mount,[24] from which these thoughts come, is itself a rich meditation on what it means for God to be our Father.

Theologian J. I. Packer suggests that there is no higher or richer description of the Christian than this: 'A Christian is one who has God as Father.'[25] By God's free grace we are sons and daughters of God. To think this way is life-transforming. To be justified and forgiven is a relief. To be adopted is a wonder.

Where justification assures us of the forgiveness of our sin, adoption assures us of a relationship of love with the one who has forgiven us. To be adopted is to be brought by God into a relationship with Him that did not exist before. It is to be welcomed into His household having all the privileges, not of a servant or of an employee, but of a son or daughter. This is a privilege that comes only to those who through faith are united with Christ.[26]

---

22 'If you then, who are evil, know how to give good gifts to your children, how much more will your Father who is in heaven give good things to those who ask him!' (Matt. 7:11).

23 'Therefore do not be anxious, saying, "What shall we eat?" or "What shall we drink?" or "What shall we wear?" For the Gentiles seek after all these things, and your heavenly Father knows that you need them all' (Matt. 6:31-2).

24 Matthew 5-7.

25 J. I. Packer, *Knowing God* (United States: InterVarsity Press, 1973, 1993), p. 200.

26 'But to all who did receive him, who believed in his name, he gave the right to become children of God' (John 1:12). In this sense it is not accurate to think of all people as the children of God. Yes, all are the offspring of His creative act. But the rich sense of fatherly

Adoption is a significant change of status which brings the Christian into all the privileges that come to children. One of those privileges is that of knowing that one will never be cast out. Children disobey and children are disciplined for their disobedience. I did things as a child that made my parents angry or sad or both. So did you. But if our parents were good parents, if our fathers were good fathers, they did not kick us out of the house and disown us because of that disobedience. We may have been disobedient children, but we were still our parents' children. God is such a good father. We are often disobedient children whom He must lovingly correct. But we are still His children and ever will be.

I once attended a hearing before a judge when a young man was adopting his new wife's eight-year-old daughter. The judge looked at this man sternly and said, 'You know this is forever, don't you? You can't change your mind and decide to undo this.'

Our heavenly Father knows that adoption is forever. He will never change His mind. Even when we disobey. A parent's love is like that.

29 THOSE SANCTIFIED

Q. 35. What is sanctification?
A. Sanctification is the work of God's free grace, whereby we are renewed in the whole man after the image of God, and are enabled more and more to die unto sin, and live unto righteousness.

care here comes only to those who by faith are united with Christ, and therefore adopted into the family of God.

The early Christians whose lives are reflected in the pages of the New Testament were a worthy bunch in many ways. Their passion and sacrifice are a model for us as they faced adversity and yet persevered. But the Bible also makes clear that they were people, imperfect and flawed like us. They argued and stretched the truth. They sometimes showed favoritism too freely and tolerated error too quickly. Much of their behavior we would not describe as saintly, and yet God was pleased to call them (and us) saints.[27] Though broken and sinful, they were united with Christ and set apart by God. As those so set apart, they were 'sanctified.' In a settled and definitive way God pronounced them 'holy.'

The problem is that they, and we who are God's holy ones, don't act like it. The *work* of God which is sanctification is a process by which Christians are enabled by God to act more and more as who they are, as God's holy people. And as Jesus is the model of holiness, sanctification is God through His Holy Spirit making His people more like Jesus. This work, this process, can be painful, and it can be slow, but it is always good.

There are sinful ways of living and reacting and behaving that come easily to us. Though we are Christians, though we are in union with Christ and so justified, adopted, and set apart as saints, these well-practiced behaviors persist. We are pulled by the world to speak falsely, to neglect compassion,

---

27 An example is the way the Bible speaks of the Corinthians, a particularly difficult bunch: 'To the church of God that is in Corinth, to those sanctified in Christ Jesus, called to be saints together with all those who in every place call upon the name of our Lord Jesus Christ, both their Lord and ours' (1 Cor. 1:2).

or to celebrate pride. We have an instinctual recourse to erupt with rage, to seek revenge, or to hoard money. We have traumatic histories or inexplicable inner urges that tempt us to sexual expressions that fall outside the biblical norm. To die to these impulses and to embrace a new way of life is incredibly hard and will never be complete before we die. And yet God is working in our lives to shape us and to conform us to the image of Christ. When we see change, we are seeing the evidence of the work of God.

The path on which God leads us as He conforms us to Christ's character looks different for all of us. Some Christians may by personality or background or fortuitous cultural influence be closer to a Christ-like demeanor than those who have suffered a lifetime of abuse and trauma. The goal of sanctification in each is the same—to be like Jesus—but reaching that goal will follow different paths over different durations of time, and each person will come to different plateaus. For all of us sanctification will be a roller-coaster ride with strides forward and strides backwards. But in it all we can never ever forget that ultimately it is not we who sanctify ourselves, but God who works in us to make us like Jesus. He began a good work in us, Paul says in Philippians, and He will see that it is completed.[28] It is His work to change us and He is doing so.

The 'mechanics' of sanctification[29] will occupy our consideration soon in these studies. At this point be heartened knowing that God is the one who is changing you. Don't despair if the progress seems slow and don't quit

---

28 'And I am sure of this, that he who began a good work in you will bring it to completion at the day of Jesus Christ' (Phil. 1:6).

29 That is, the answer to the question of 'What then do I do?'

because it is hard. A verse of the Christmas hymn 'It Came upon a Midnight Clear' uses the language of John Milton to acknowledge that the walk of the Christian is never easy.

> *And ye, beneath life's crushing load,*
> *whose forms are bending low,*
> *who toil along the climbing way*
> *with painful steps and slow....*[30]

The steps of sanctification are often wandering, painful, and slow. But they are guided by a wise and good God, our heavenly Father, who is willing even now to call you—as He did those early, irascible Christians—holy.

---

30 Edmund H. Sears, 'It Came upon a Midnight Clear' *The Trinity Hymnal, Revised Edition*, #200.

6

The Promise of the Future

When my mother died, her children were shocked to see the extent of the estate she left. Her will detailed an inheritance for each of us that was far greater than any of us had dreamed.

The first portion of the Catechism has outlined for us 'what we are to believe concerning God.' Here at the end we are hearing read for us a will in which we who are Christians are the beneficiaries. The details of our inheritance are far greater than any of us could have dreamed.

It is true that we do not yet possess all that is ours to receive. And yet these things are certain. As Peter puts it, the Christian's inheritance is 'an inheritance that is imperishable, undefiled, and unfading, kept in heaven for you.'[1]

The details of that inheritance are what we will now consider. Know that along with being rich beyond our dreams, this inheritance is kept safe and it is surely to be ours.

---

1   1 Peter 1:4.

30 BENEFITS

> Q. 36. What are the benefits which in this life do accompany or flow from justification, adoption and sanctification?
>
> A. The benefits which in this life do accompany or flow from justification, adoption and sanctification, are, assurance of God's love, peace of conscience, joy in the Holy Ghost, increase of grace, and perseverance therein to the end.

One Christmas our daughter, Adria, and her husband, Gamaliel, gave Barb and me a new board game. The box contained several distinct types of cards, different kinds of markers by which points would be calculated, and various pieces that actually were to be moved around the board. With these came a twelve-page booklet outlining the rules, suggesting strategy, and detailing the method for calculating points. Our minds were spinning.

Until we actually played the game. Then we began to understand what had been mere words on a page and items on a table.

The theology we have been studying may feel the same. Words on a page. Distant, abstract, confusing. Until we are engaged in the game.

Justification, adoption, and sanctification are merely ideas until, as we have tried to show, they are experienced as lifting our guilt, giving us family, and assuring our transformation. Theology is meant to intersect with life, which is the point of this summary question and answer. Detailed here is a brief catalog of the vast implications of the Christian's union with Christ. Theology is not abstract, but reveals for us the promises of assurance and peace, of joy, and of grace and perseverance, all good gifts of God flowing from our union through justification, adoption, and sanctification. These are rich benefits to which we can only here afford a glimpse.

Consider the assurance of God's love. Christians all come to a place where they question it. When good people get cancer or when guilty people get away with awful crimes, we question, if not blame, God. How can these things come from a loving God? We ought not to measure God's love by circumstances but by the cross. The fact of the cross does not change. God gave His Son to deliver us from evil.[2] It is in His work at the cross that His love is objectively revealed.[3] We need not doubt it, even in the face of things we cannot understand.

But then our hearts condemn us. We try to follow Jesus, but we stumble and fall. We curse the guy who cut us off in traffic or we click on the wrong internet sites or tell an untruth to get ahead in our job, or worse. We hate that we do these things and we feel guilty for them and we begin to feel the weight of self-condemnation. But we need not despair. Peace of conscience flows from our justification, adoption, and sanctification. Jesus' righteousness is ours, we are God's forgiven and beloved children, and we are being made to be more like Jesus. Breathe these things in and be at peace.

---

2   '…who gave himself for our sins to deliver us from the present evil age, according to the will of our God and Father…' (Gal. 1:4).

3   '…but God shows his love for us in that while we were still sinners, Christ died for us' (Rom. 5:8).

And be joyful. In a world that is not all that it is supposed to be, we can see that God has done a work that secures our future. That work is done. We can experience shafts of joy in this broken world when we call to mind His presence and work. Joy is a blessing and a gift.

And we find joy in the fact that we are not left where we were found. God continues to pour grace into our lives. His Spirit nurtures us through the wandering steps of life and reminds us of all the truths that impact us.

Which leads to our perseverance. There may be mountains and valleys before us, but God enables us, again by grace, to confidently persevere in His favor to the end, a glorious destination, the nature of which we will next consider.

So, yes. This is theology. These are words on the page. This may feel like the rules to a game we have not yet played. But once the game is engaged, once we live our lives in the light of our union with Christ and the vast impact of all that means, these words become the words of life itself.

31 DEATH

> Q. 37. What benefits do believers receive from Christ at death?
> A. The souls of believers are at their death made perfect in holiness, and do immediately pass into glory; and their bodies, being still united to Christ, do rest in their graves till the resurrection.

We think about death a lot.

One Friday evening, Barb and I watched a television episode in which two of the main characters found themselves in a sealed container on the ocean floor.[4] As scientists they had calculated how long they would survive given the limited oxygen they had available. This led them to contemplate what lies beyond death. They concluded they would decompose and nothing more. It was a silly show, but the question raised and the answer given were serious.

The next day, we re-watched the final installment of the eight Harry Potter movies. In it Harry asked the ghosts of his ancestors what death is like. 'Quicker than going to sleep,' he is told. It was a quick scene, but revealing. Even the audience for Harry Potter movies is thinking about death.

Death weighs on us because, in fact, we are all dying.[5]

There is little I can say to soften the pain of loss and struggle that is death, and there is much that is mysterious in it. What I can say is that as believers, even in death, we are held safely by God.[6]

Death overwhelms us with loss, and so we fear it. It is, the Bible says, an enemy.[7] It casts a cloud over life and in the end it rips apart what God created to be whole. Soul is torn from body in an unnatural separation. Can we speak of any

---

4   *Agents of S.H.I.E.L.D*, Season 1, Episode 22.

5   That death occupies the contemplations of philosophers, we have already noted. See Q/A 32.

6   Jesus in the Gospel of John gives us this assurance: 'I give them eternal life, and they will never perish, and no one will snatch them out of my hand. My Father, who has given them to me, is greater than all, and no one is able to snatch them out of the Father's hand. I and the Father are one' (John 10:28-30).

7   'The last enemy to be destroyed is death' (1 Cor. 15:26).

benefit arising from such a thing? We can because Christ has, in His death and resurrection, transformed death for the Christian.

In death the soul of the believer, that part of the human in which consciousness rests, does not cease to exist but passes into 'glory.' What is this glory? It is an existence with Jesus in what He calls paradise.[8] The joy of it is that we are with Him, the one we love. There the Christian will find the perfection she has longed for. She will find an immediacy of contentment as the struggle for holiness is brought to an end and she is welcomed into the presence of the Savior who loved and sought her.

But there is more. The unnatural rending of body and soul is not forever. As we are united with Christ, we are united with Him body and soul, as whole persons. Our bodies will lie in the grave, whether we die of natural causes or are burned in a fire, and will remain united with Christ. There will come a time when our bodies will be raised and renewed, as Christ's was. Then will the work of redemption be complete, and there death will meet its final defeat.[9]

Death is an awful thing. A terrible thing. A thing unnatural and contrary to the original creation of God and something in life we will think often about.

Kurt Vonnegut's narrator in his novel, *Slaughterhouse-Five*, confronts the inevitability of death, saying 'so it goes' whenever death is mentioned. The repetition seems to 'deaden' us to the concerns associated with death. So it goes.

---

8   As Jesus said to a repentant thief crucified next to him: 'Truly, I say to you, today you will be with me in paradise' (Luke 23:43).

9   See the next section on Q/A 38.

But we need not greet death with such a shoulder shrug nor with fear. Death does not win. Death is inevitable but not the end. We endure death, in Christ, because even in death God does not let us go.

32 JOY

> Q. 38. What benefits do believers receive from Christ at the resurrection?
>
> A. At the resurrection, believers being raised up in glory, shall be openly acknowledged and acquitted in the day of judgment, and made perfectly blessed in the full enjoying of God to all eternity.

'Daddy, if I get eaten by a bear, will I still go to heaven?'

That and 'Will there be bathrooms in heaven?' are two of the many questions about heaven that my kids have asked over the years. The Bible assures Christians of life after death, but the nature of that life is only revealed in rough outline. Nevertheless what we are told is breathtaking. We will behold and be with God, which will be our greatest joy.

Death is not the end of life. And life after death is not the end for which people are created. Time moves forward toward what is called 'the resurrection.' There will come a time when the bodies of the dead will be raised and reunited with their souls, which have awaited this time with the risen

Jesus.[10] It does not matter if in life that body was confined to a wheelchair or a bed. It does not matter whether the person dies from length of days or from stepping on a land mine. At the resurrection the body will rise, similar to the body that was but made new. The only model we have of this is the way the resurrected body of Jesus was the same but at the same time new. But the point here is that eternity will be a bodily existence. We will not strum harps on clouds, and we will not sprout wings or become angels. We will be the human person we always have been, though made perfect. Believers will be openly declared really and finally righteous. Our redemption, what Jesus came to accomplish, will be complete. All struggle will cease.

But complete for what? If the resurrection of the body is the consummation of all for which Jesus died, then what will it be like? God has revealed less on this point than much human speculation might think. Often our human hope of heaven terminates with an expectation of being reunited with loved ones. That is wonderful, but it is woefully incomplete and insufficient. The greatest joy of heaven will be the full enjoying of God. We will 'behold him as he is'[11] and in that beholding find joy to all eternity. The richest blessing of heaven will be our finding our hearts' greatest happiness, fullness, and contentment in God. We will find in seeing Jesus and being with Him a complete and unending happiness.

10　'Behold! I tell you a mystery. We shall not all sleep, but we shall all be changed, in a moment, in the twinkling of an eye, at the last trumpet. For the trumpet will sound, and the dead will be raised imperishable, and we shall be changed' (1 Cor. 15:51-2).

11　1 John 3:2.

When the Apostle Paul considers eternity, he revels in the fact that he will be 'with Christ.'[12] The psalmist Asaph muses that, as there is 'nothing on Earth that I desire besides' God, so he rests in the hope that God would be his 'portion forever.'[13] If we were created, as the first question and answer beautifully affirm, 'to enjoy [God] forever' then this glorious end is what our hearts were created for. We will find our deepest human calling fulfilled in the full enjoying of God to all eternity. We will be happy in Him, and perfectly content. Forever.

Philosophers and students of human psychology have questioned whether sustained happiness is possible. It is very difficult for us to conceive of a life without conflict and struggle. But to be perfectly blessed is to be perfectly content and in possession of all that our hearts have longed for. We will be happy in Him. The greatest joy of heaven is not golden streets or having life's puzzling questions finally answered. The greatest joy, the realization that will elicit from us sighs of the deepest satisfaction, is that we will be present with our loving God in unfettered and unmediated happiness.

Even if we once had been eaten by a bear.

---

12 'My desire is to depart and be with Christ, for that is far better' (Phil. 1:23).

13 'Whom have I in heaven but you?
And there is nothing on earth that I desire besides you.
My flesh and my heart may fail,
      but God is the strength of my heart and my portion forever' (Ps. 73:25-6).

Part 2
Life Worth Living

You will remember that the Catechism answered the question, 'What do the Scriptures principally teach?' with two broad considerations, 'The Scriptures principally teach what man is to believe concerning God, and what duty God requires of man.'

It is this second division to which we now turn our attention. The duty God requires is mapped out along three pathways.

First, the Catechism introduces us to the law of God. In the law we are given the direction in which we can best glorify and enjoy God as well as find our greatest happiness.

But the law also exposes the rebellious character of the human heart. So the Catechism will help us consider how we, by grace, respond to this reality through faith and repentance.

And finally, the Catechism guides us in how we might live lives of faithfullness in a world that challenges and opposes us. It coaxes us to draw near to the God who loves us and gave us life in His Son, through the Church, its sacraments,[1] and prayer.

---

1   'Sacrament' is an ancient word used by Christians to speak of those Christian practices that have a special purpose of revealing to believers the goodness and grace and favor of God. These

This, the Catechism says, is the duty God requires.

But this word 'duty' is a difficult and an unhappy one for many. If salvation is free, why then must we talk of duty? The word feels oppressive and restrictive. And yet duty need not be. Duty in response to love becomes behavior happily chosen. Yes, Scripture prescribes pathways of obedience. But these are pathways to guide us in ways that our hearts want to go. What could be oppressive is transformed into joy when we are aware that the one prescribing our obedience is the one who has loved us. It is important that the Catechism has exposed for us first the grace we have been given by God. It is this 'indicative,' this statement of the way things are— God's love for us—that moves our 'imperative,' the duty we are given by which we show our love for Him in return.

In the movie *Hachi: A Dog's Tale*, Richard Gere plays an urban professor of music who routinely takes the train from his suburban home to the college where he teaches. His dog, Hachi, follows him to the train station every day and waits for his return, sitting like a sentinel until his master gets off the train. No one ever told Hachi to behave this way. He was not forced to do it. Hachi's strong desire was born of his love for and devotion to his master. What he seemed to do as a duty was behavior freely chosen arising from that love-birthed devotion.

Duty so conceived hardly seems like duty at all. It becomes a path freely chosen in response to our master's love for us.

---

sacraments, baptism and the Lord's Supper, will be explored in Chapter Eleven.

7
Obedience and Love

Law can be a gift we fail to appreciate adequately. At a recent choral concert I was frustrated that there was no law given regarding cell phones. As a result people used their phones to film the concert, to illuminate their program, and, in one case at least, to read a book. Many just did not consider how distracting their cell phone use might be to others like myself. A properly framed law would have been helpful to make the concert a happier experience for everyone.

God's law can be appreciated in this way. It is not, as some might think, an imposition by an oppressive tyrant looking to eliminate all fun from the world. It is rather a gift from a kind and loving Creator whose desire is our happiness. We can see this in at least three ways.[1]

First, the law is a gift which benefits the world at large by providing an objective standard of right and wrong, a measure by which good and evil might be distinguished and society most happily ordered. These standards find application in society whether or not that society acknowledges or appreciates their source. Expectations of honesty and prohibitions against theft are common societal

---

1   In theological terms, these are known as the three 'uses' of the law.

norms that help order society. At root, these standards arise from the gift of God's law.

The law is also a gift to the sinner. These commandments can awaken the sensitive conscience to the depth of sin and the need of a savior. The law moves people to seek out Christ. As hard as this might be for some, it is a gift.

As well, the law is a particular gift of love to the Christian. The law, as we have already suggested, shows us how Christians can respond to the great grace we have been shown. Grace moves us to *want* to love God. The law shows us how.

It is this understanding of the law as a gift that prompts people like the psalmist David to say: 'Oh, how I love your law.'[2] That may not yet be your response. I hope it soon shall be.

33 FOR OUR OWN GOOD

> Q. 39. What is the duty which God requires of man?
> A. The duty which God requires of man is obedience to his revealed will.

> Q. 40. What did God at first reveal to man for the rule of his obedience?
> A. The rule which God at first revealed to man for his obedience was the moral law.

---

2   Psalm 119:97.

Adrian was a college friend who was Luna Lovegood before Luna Lovegood was cool.[3] She was a free spirit and an independent thinker and, as too often is the case, was frequently alone. Adrian was above all a thoughtful Christian who one day, standing with me at a crosswalk waiting for traffic to clear, gave me a life altering take on God's commandments. 'What if,' she pondered, 'God gave us these laws for our own good?' There was much more to that conversation, but it changed the way I looked at God's law.

But first we need to think about what in fact constitutes God's law. The Catechism makes clear in Q/A 3 that this law is revealed in the Bible, but how? The Bible seems full of commandments, some of which are clearly applicable to us (such as restraining our tongue) and others which seem remote and obscure (such as how a priest is commanded to dress for the Day of Atonement).

Wisely, the Catechism narrows our focus to the moral law. Jesus Himself was a faithful follower of the moral law, and that His followers should do the same is no surprise. But this begs the question. What is the moral law? Before we can isolate it, we need to distinguish the *moral* law from the *ceremonial* law (having to do with how worship was to be conducted before Jesus' death and resurrection) and the *civil* law (having to do with how Israel was to be governed). It is the moral law that maps out our duty and is given for our good.

---

3   If you are unfamiliar with Luna Lovegood from J. K. Rowling's Harry Potter books, your life is diminished, but you will not lose the thrust of my point.

But the map can be blurred by well-intentioned people. The moral law revealed in Scripture must be distinguished from the 'laws' people add through tradition or the concerns of their particular cultural moment. That I not steal my neighbor's car is revealed in Scripture. That I wear a tie to church or avoid red dye #2 is not.

Even when we are able to isolate in Scripture what *seems* to be a moral commandment (such as '…be fruitful and multiply…'[4]), how are we to know how to properly apply this to our lives? That is an important question for the Christian who loves God and longs to obey Him.

Left to ourselves, knowing what to obey and how to obey can be quite confusing. Left to ourselves what is meant to be for our own good can begin to feel overwhelming and oppressive.

Happily we are not left to ourselves.

Wise men and women of the past who have lived life well and who have reflected on the careful and sensitive application of biblical truth to real life in a variety of settings and cultures point the way for us. The Catechism is in this sense a repository of this received wisdom of the past. It will not answer every question, and we continue to need wise teachers with a careful approach to Scripture to help us. And yet the Catechism stands in this tradition of elders to give us guidance as to how to isolate and to understand the commandments of God. With this help we will begin to see, with my friend Adrian, how the law—in particular the Commandments—is given for our own good.

---

4   Genesis 1:22, 28; 8:17, etc.

34 THE DEFINITION OF LOVE

Q. 41. Where is the moral law summarily comprehended?
A. The moral law is summarily comprehended in the Ten Commandments.

Q. 42. What is the sum of the Ten Commandments?
A. The sum of the Ten Commandments is to love the Lord our God with all our heart, with all our soul, with all our strength, and with all our mind; and our neighbor as ourselves.

In his novel *The Plague*, Albert Camus presents a noble and appealing character. Caught in a town overrun by bubonic plague, he serves selflessly at the risk of his own life. These are people he hardly knows, and yet he plunges into their suffering in order to find ways to bring relief. In a very profound way, he shows what it means to love. And if there is a way to summarize the moral law of God, it would be to say that by it God shows us how to love.

The moral law, touched upon in many places in the Bible, is given its clearest expression in what is known as the 'Ten Commandments.' These were given by God through Moses and recorded for us in the Bible in the twentieth chapter of Exodus and repeated in the fifth chapter of Deuteronomy. It is these ten that the Catechism will now seek to unpack and apply for us.

According to Jesus the heart of these Commandments can be summarized by the word 'love.' This in itself is unsurprising since most ethical systems end up with some expression of 'love' at their core. As Camus' character reveals, such systems can do a lot of good in the world. Motivated by love, the poor are fed, the ill are treated, and lost car keys are returned to their owners.

And yet those systems are incomplete in ways the Bible is not. Love, as Jesus and the Commandments direct us, aims in two necessary and complementary directions. We are to love God and love others. While other systems might speak well of loving one's neighbor, they will neglect the duty of loving God. Further, the simple call to love is terribly vague. The word 'love' itself is a container so vast that anyone can pour into it whatever definition seems to suit the moment.[5]

So, we need the Commandments to guide us in love. They show us how to love both God and neighbor.

The first four commandments give shape to how we love God. We love God, even when we are struggling to feel what we should toward Him, by worshiping Him only, in the way He commands, with purity of devotion, and in a rhythm of remembrance.

We are guided by the final six commandments to love our neighbors well, even those for whom we lack warm feelings, by honoring authority, by treating others' lives and health as

---

5   Or, as N. T. Wright memorably put it: 'The English word "love" is trying to do so many different jobs at the same time that someone really ought to sit down with it and teach it how to delegate.' *After You Believe: Why Christian Character Matters* (United States: HarperCollins, 2010), p. 183.

something of value, by acting honorably toward others, by respecting their property, and by being honest with them.

In the end, what it means to love is not a mystery. The Commandments point us to the path of loving God and others. Walking that path may or may not qualify the traveler for sainthood, as Camus pondered in his book. But if she is on this path, sainthood is not her goal. God is.

35 BOUND BY LOVE

Q. 43. What is the preface to the Ten Commandments?
A. The preface to the Ten Commandments is in these words, I am the LORD your God, who brought you out of the land of Egypt, out of the house of slavery.

Q. 44. What does the preface to the Ten Commandments teach us?
A. The preface to the Ten Commandments teaches us that because God is the Lord, and our God, and redeemer, therefore we are bound to keep all his commandments.

The Catechism here says that Christians are 'bound' to keep God's commandments. This raises a question we have already touched upon.[6] Are we 'bound'? Or are we free? It is odd, at the very least, to say that we are bound, when

---

6   See the introduction to Part Two.

the words from which that is drawn speaks of being set free from slavery. So which is it? Are we free or are we bound?

That we are most wondrously free was the theme of Part One. As a child of God we are free to come before our Father and speak to Him.[7] We are free to fail and to stumble and to fall, for our salvation is a free gift of God's grace, secured by the righteousness of Christ.[8] We were those bound to death, 'dead in the trespasses and sins'[9], and captured by 'the domain of darkness.'[10] Now all of that is behind us. We are out of the reach of such things, united with Christ in a salvation 'imperishable, undefiled, and unfading, kept in heaven for you.'[11] Our bondage to sin has been broken, and great gifts we could never earn have been given.[12] Like Israel being released from Egypt, we are free.

We are free, and yet we are never without a king. Even in the most trivial way, we all choose to serve a lawgiver. As a free man, when I determine to have relationships with other humans, I bind myself to certain rules, not the least of which being that I will need to bathe now and then. The commandments of social intercourse require it, and this becomes the king I serve. We may be free, but we will always find a king to serve.

Not all kings are freely chosen. Were an armed gunman to enter a coffee shop and demand compliance of me and those around me, we would for a time be under his kingship. We

---

7   Q/A 34, 'Those Adopted'.

8   Q/A 33, 'Those Justified'.

9   Ephesians 2:1.

10 Colossians 1:13.

11 1 Peter 1:4.

12 Q/A 32, 'Those Blessed'.

would follow his rules, but we would long for someone to deliver us. If delivered, we would look with deep gratitude upon our deliverer.

Those who received the Ten Commandments at Mount Sinai had been subjects against their will of a king they did not want. They had been bound in the most restrictive way by the most unrighteous and unwelcome rule. When God freed Israel from this bondage and formed them into a nation, He became their new king. As such, He gave them a law by which they could flourish. They were bound to Him, a benevolent king, but their bondage in this case was a response of gratitude and love.

This is the pattern by which we as Christians are to understand our own relationship to God and to His law. Through Jesus God has delivered us from 'the domain of darkness' as we noted. But He has also 'transferred us to the kingdom of his beloved son.'[13] A kingdom has a king, and a king is one who rules. We have a new king, but one who rules with a desire for our flourishing, and we can trust Him to lead us well. To Him we are bound, but willingly. Sometimes the law by which He rules seems sensible and sometimes it feels arbitrary. But always obedience is called for. We are bound to the God we trust. He is our redeemer first and then our king.

Perhaps you are familiar with Dobby the house elf in the magical world of J. K. Rowling's Harry Potter books. House elves were slaves, bound to do their master's will. They were often abused and rarely set free. But through a series of events, Harry Potter was able to set Dobby free.

---

13   Colossians 1:13.

What did Dobby do with his new freedom? At a critical point of the story Dobby defies the powerful with these words: 'Dobby is a free elf and Dobby has come to save Harry Potter and his friends!'[14] Dobby was free and in that freedom bound himself to his deliverer.

So, are we free or are we bound?

The answer is, 'Yes.'

---

14   J. K. Rowling, *Harry Potter and the Deathly Hallows* (United States: Scholastic Inc., 2007), p. 474.

8

How to Love God

God created people and those He created find their greatest joy in loving Him. Sin, however, leads us to love all the wrong things in all the wrong ways. And so God acted to rescue us from all those false loves and the deep unhappiness that arises from them. That is, as the Catechism has expressed it, He redeemed His people from their sin and misery.

But a rescued people do not immediately learn *how* to love God, even though they may want to do so. The first four commandments reveal how people are to love God in the way that most pleases Him and in the way that brings to them—to we who are the redeemed—the deepest satisfaction. Here we are shown the channels in which our actions should flow in order for our hearts to be directed in the way they were created to go.

But we still resist.

When I was a young piano student, I failed to appreciate how conformity to law would one day give me freedom and joy. I was taught to sit a certain way, to hold my hands a certain way, and, hardest of all, to be constrained by the incessant 'tick, tick, tick, tick' of the metronome. I resisted these laws even though they were designed by my teacher to set me free to love the piano. As a result, a piano sits in a room of our house largely silent. The beauty that was possible is not realized.

These commandments are designed to give us freedom to enjoy the beauty that is God and to live most happily as His people. They enable us to love as we were created to love.

36 THE OBJECT OF LOVE

Q. 45. Which is the first commandment?
A. The first commandment is,
You shall have no other gods before me.

Q. 46. What is required in the first commandment?
A. The first commandment requires us to know and acknowledge God to be the only true God, and our God; and to worship and glorify him accordingly.

Q. 47. What is forbidden in the first commandment?
A. The first commandment forbids the denying, or not worshiping and glorifying the true God as God, and our God; and the giving of that worship and glory to any other, which is due to him alone.

> Q. 48. What are we specially taught by these words
> 'before me' in the first commandment?
> A. These words 'before me' in the first commandment
> teach us that God, who sees all things, takes notice of,
> and is much displeased with, the sin of having any other
> god.

What God requires in the First Commandment is for people to worship Him only. Why, we wonder, is this okay for God when we know that such a trait when seen in our peers is odious?

It is okay for God because God, being unlike anything or anyone else, only requires what is proper, and what is necessary, for us.

We must not forget that God alone is the infinite, eternal, and unchangeable God, the Creator of all that there is. We are created things; He is not. Before the glory and majesty and greatness of the Creator we are as nothing. When we think of Him as simply an elevated expression of humanity, we think of Him wrongly and our thinking is impoverished. In fact, whenever people in the Bible were granted a glimpse of His glory, they often fell to their faces in fear and worship. He is the one, holy God and there is no other. To place the honor that He should receive elsewhere would be to honor a falsehood and to distort what ought to be. To worship Him and no other is the only worship that is proper.

Far from being an odious demand, it is merciful.

It is merciful because our deepest happiness comes when we make the true God our only God. The fall was triggered by the lie that we could find happiness elsewhere. This commandment mercifully directs us back and keeps us where we ought to be. We are created to worship Him and to find our greatest joy in Him. Those who settle for less not only fall under condemnation for committing a grievous offense against the holy God, they are to be pitied as those who are greatly diminished in life. They are like the person standing on a mountain peak but unable to appreciate the view because he finally got cell coverage and is consumed with social media posts on his phone. This commandment demands as well as invites us to lift our eyes and our devotion to where true beauty and happiness reside.

But what are the false gods who distract us? A false god is anything we value in the place of the true God. They are many and are normally not identified by churches, temples, or shrines. They are often the good things to which we give an outsized portion of our devotion. In the western world we elevate things like family and country, freedom and property, all good things, to a level that trumps our devotion to God. When asked to give away our goods as an act of worship, we hesitate. When called to speak up for God at the cost of our reputation we shrink back. The temptations to deny the true God as God come to us often, and we too often fail.

Our failure reminds us that in the end no other god but He is worthy of our devotion. For no other god shows the mercy He does. To worship this God only is not only proper, it is our joy.

37 THE WAY OF LOVE

Q. 49. Which is the second commandment?
A. The second commandment is,
You shall not make for yourself a carved image, or any likeness of anything that is in heaven above, or that is in the earth beneath, or that is in the water under the earth. You shall not bow down to them or serve them, for I the LORD your God am a jealous God, visiting the iniquity of the fathers on the children to the third and the fourth generation of those who hate me, but showing steadfast love to thousands of those who love me and keep my commandments.

Q. 50. What is required in the second commandment?
A. The second commandment requires the receiving, observing, and keeping pure and entire, all such religious worship and ordinances as God has appointed in his Word.

Q. 51. What is forbidden in the second commandment?
A. The second commandment forbids the worshiping of God by images, or any other way not appointed in his Word.

> Q. 52. What are the reasons annexed to the second commandment?
> A. The reasons annexed to the second commandment are, God's sovereignty over us, his propriety in us, and the zeal he has to his own worship.

The Commandments, we must remember, were not given to people as individuals. They were given to a nation. This nation was a community, a people gathered together around the one true God. The Commandments, that is, were given to a church, to God's gathered people, and they were intended to shape the life of that church. The first commandment directs the community, the church, to worship God only. The second commandment directs the way in which that community should express that worship. For the Christian, the second commandment directs the character of our Sunday morning worship.[1] There are ways we worship that honor the true God and ways that dishonor Him. Sometimes even the best of people cannot tell the difference. This commandment would have us make sure that worship is given shape by Scripture.

When Moses was away on Mount Sinai receiving the law from God, Moses' brother Aaron led the newly delivered slaves in an act of worship. Their intentions were right. They

---

1   The second commandment has public worship, not public art, in view. Some (including some of those who wrote this Catechism) have extrapolated this command to forbid the painting of pictures of Jesus or in other ways to constrain artistic expression. I am of the conviction that only public worship is in the commandment's view and so I restrict my comments to that end.

offered their worship to the right God, the God who had delivered them from Egypt. But they shaped their worship by their own cultural background (they were all raised in Egypt) and did not allow that background to be processed with guidance from God. They chose to worship Him in the form of a created thing, a golden calf. They did not wait to learn how to shape their worship by the revelation of God. As a result, instead of honoring God, they diminished the glory of God and their worship was condemned.[2] We want to honor God in worship and the only way to do that is to shape our worship by Scripture.

Having Scripture to guide us allows us to worship God in a way that is 'pure and entire' and enables us to avoid acts of worship 'not appointed in his Word.' That said, we must embrace some humility as we move forward in applying these things. Clarity on what arises from these directives is not always easy to come by. The definitions of what is 'appointed' and what is 'pure' require careful thought steeped in Scripture. It also requires more liberty than we sometimes want to give. Wars literal and wars figurative have been fought over what should and should not be a part of Christian worship.

Some Christians believe that to have crosses or other imagery in Christian worship is to violate the second commandment. Others believe that such symbols are not worshiped and are useful to enhance devotion. Some believe that Scripture permits only the singing of psalms while others believe that songs of human composition are not only permitted but essential. Some believe musical instruments

---

2   Exodus 32:1-4.

are a gift to be used in worship and others oppose them as lacking in scriptural warrant. We could go on. Clarity is not always easy. Christians will differ.

Certainly scriptural worship is a deeply serious thing. Nadab and Abihu were condemned for offering to the Lord what was deemed 'strange fire,' an act not commanded.[3] But such seriousness does not exclude the spontaneous and creative. Miriam danced before the Lord[4] and Joshua erected a pile of rocks as a worshipful remembrance of God's merciful acts.[5] The festival of Purim developed in response to God's providential preservation of the people through the courage of Esther.[6] These things were spontaneous, and as they are recorded in Scripture they give us scriptural warrant for some element of creativity in our worship.

Worship that is according to the Scriptures is worship structured around prayer, the reading of Scripture, preaching, song, and sacrament.[7] It is worship oriented to the glory of God providing an outlet for worshipers to give expression to how the gospel has impacted their hearts. As such it will have spontaneous and creative elements.

God, according to Scripture, is not displeased when His people, out of love and appreciation for Him, develop heartfelt and creative ways of celebrating His goodness. It pleases Him when His people come in sincerity of heart with the language and gifting of their culture to remember

---

3   Leviticus 10:1.

4   Exodus 15:19-21.

5   Joshua 4:1-10.

6   Esther 9:27-28.

7   That is, baptism and the Lord's Supper. These we will explore in Chapter Eleven.

His great works of creation, providence, and redemption. Such worship is according to Scripture.

We are pulled and tugged to worship in ways that are formed by our preferences and backgrounds. The structure of worship is therefore not to be our individual decision. The elders of the church should structure worship with careful attention to Scripture and a deep appreciation for how the Church in history has understood Scripture. As well they should carefully match what they learn to the culture and language and ways of the worshipers.

Such worship will be 'according to the Scriptures' and with this God will be honored. More than this, He will be pleased.

38 THE ATTITUDE OF LOVE

Q. 53. Which is the third commandment?
A. The third commandment is,
You shall not take the name of the LORD your God in vain, for the LORD will not hold him guiltless who takes his name in vain.

Q. 54. What is required in the third commandment?
A. The third commandment requires the holy and reverent use of God's names, titles, attributes, ordinances, word and works.

> Q. 55. What is forbidden in the third commandment?
> A. The third commandment forbids all profaning or abusing of anything whereby God makes himself known.

> Q. 56. What is the reason annexed to the third commandment?
> A. The reason annexed to the third commandment is that however the breakers of this commandment may escape punishment from men, yet the Lord our God will not suffer them to escape his righteous judgment.

The first commandment asks us to consider who or what we make ultimate in our lives and calls us to serve and worship only the living and true God. The second commandment asks us to consider how we worship that living and true God and calls us to shape our worship by Scripture alone. This commandment asks us to consider the place of our hearts in that worship, calling us to worship with sincerity. To say this, however, can trip up the struggling Christian who sometimes knows he is supposed to worship but does not feel like going to church. Is such a person condemned?

That is, just what does this commandment forbid?

It does not condemn the struggling Christian. It rather forbids dishonest pretending.

Worship that is pleasing to God is worship in which the worshiper's external acts are matched by his heart's sincere desire. To 'take the name' of God is to invoke His name as an act of appeal or honor. To invoke His name 'in vain' is to do so in an empty and meaningless way. Jesus speaks of those who honor God 'with their lips, but their heart is far' from Him.[8] This is pretend worship. It is worship with one's fingers crossed behind one's back. In human relationships we call this flattery and it aims toward manipulation. It is fake and false and condemned by God.

Pretend honor is condemned in worship, but in all other contexts as well. To swear by God's name in court when intending to lie is to pretend to honor Him. Or, to claim a relationship with God that does not exist in order to gain business contacts or political votes is to use His name dishonestly. This commandment speaks to all such situations and others like them. Forbidden is any act of pretended honor, in worship or outside of it.

And yet, does this sweeping and understandable condemnation catch in its net the struggling Christian who goes to church some Sunday when he does not want to do so? When such a Christian worships God with her lips when her body would rather be in bed, is she condemned? Does the one who goes through the motions of worship but feels like he doesn't get anything out of it risk the judgment of God?

It is good to ask such questions, but those who do so should relax. They transgress no law. God knows the orientation of the heart.

The one who worships out of obedience is welcome even though she is struggling. Her worship is not in vain, even though her emotions are out of sync with what she is doing.

---

8   Matthew 15:8.

The orientation of her life is toward God and that is pleasing to Him. Hers is a ship that knows its harbor, but has been blown off course. By worship the bow once again is set right. This is what worship is for.

Sometimes Christians fall into depression or other dark places. They desperately need the support of other Christians singing and confessing around them to keep their weak spirits alive. Their hearts feel empty and need others to hold them up. Such worship is never pretend. It is hungry, and it is obedient, but it is not in vain.

To use Jesus' name as an exclamation, or for political or business gain, or in any other empty way, is a misuse. But to take His name on our lips as a cry for help and mercy, and as worship, is exactly what we are called to do. Even, at times, when we don't feel like it.

39 THE RHYTHM OF LOVE

Q. 57. Which is the fourth commandment?
A. The fourth commandment is,
Remember the Sabbath day, to keep it holy. Six days you shall labor, and do all your work, but the seventh day is a Sabbath to the LORD your God. On it you shall not do any work, you, or your son, or your daughter, your male servant, or your female servant, or your livestock, or the sojourner who is within your gates. For in six days the LORD made heaven and earth, the sea, and all that is in them, and rested on the seventh day. Therefore the LORD blessed the Sabbath day and made it holy.

> Q. 58. What is required in the fourth commandment?
> A. The fourth commandment requires the keeping holy to God such set times as he has appointed in his Word; expressly one whole day in seven, to be a holy Sabbath to himself.

> Q. 59. Which day of the seven has God appointed to be the weekly Sabbath?
> A. From the beginning of the world to the resurrection of Christ, God appointed the seventh day of the week to be the weekly Sabbath; and the first day of the week ever since, to continue to the end of the world, which is the Christian Sabbath.

A year, the amount of time it takes for the earth to make one complete trip around the sun, is an astronomical reality. The earth's tilt on its axis fixes those seasons we know as Spring, Summer, Fall, and Winter. When the earth completes one rotation on that axis, we mark it as a day. A month, in some calendars, is linked to the phases of the moon.

But a week as a measure of time is linked to no physical reality. There is no astronomical event that sets it at seven days and not eight (as the Romans once observed) or ten. Though a week roughly approximates a fourth of a lunar cycle, it does not seem to have appeared because of that. Why do we speak of a week at all, and why do we set it at seven days?

We do so solely because God has decreed it to be the defining rhythm for creatures created in His image. God created in six days and rested on the seventh. A week is not an astronomical reality but a human need defined by our Creator's pattern. Though God did not need rest, He knew His creatures would. He set the rhythm we now mark.

This rhythm serves a physical need and it addresses a spiritual one. Those who work and rarely stop (true of many Americans) not only grow weary from the harm to their bodies, the physical cost, but they also develop a false sense of self-sufficiency, the spiritual cost. To work without rest allows us to believe that we carry the full responsibility for our lives. God is reduced by such self-sufficiency to a talisman invoked in desperation rather than the provider He truly is. Our hearts are drawn away from Him to our spiritual depletion. The practice of one day of rest in seven, the rhythm of the week, is a gift of God to serve our bodies and our hearts.

One Sunday in college, feeling the pressure of all that I was never going to get done, I threw the book I was reading across the room in desperation. What on the outside appeared to be a stress-relieving outburst was in reality a creaturely cry for rest, my inner desire for sabbath. My subsequent decision to stop working Sundays, which as a student meant no studying, was counter-intuitive but felt necessary. It came with surprising results. Sundays suddenly became days of great joy. I now had time for worship and for friends and for rest. Oddly my work somehow still got done. And my faith blossomed as I was conscious of being less dependent on my own efforts and more dependent upon God. Learning to make 'one whole day in seven' a 'holy sabbath' to God, something with which I continue to struggle, is a deeply formative thing.

In the Jewish context of the commandment, the seventh day began at sundown on our Friday and extended until sundown on Saturday. Sunday was not the seventh day but the first. And yet, the vast majority of Christians seem to ignore this obvious historic reality and practice Sunday as the Sabbath, or Lord's Day. We do so because of the cataclysmic impact of the resurrection of Jesus. He rose from the dead on the first day of the week. When Scripture records His appearances thereafter, they are always on the first day. The practice of Christians resting on the first day, not the seventh, is traceable to, and in celebration of, the resurrection of Jesus.

Upon reflection, this is no surprise. The resurrection of Jesus is the natural fulfillment of the sabbath idea. There is a rest, a sabbath rest, awaiting us all in heaven. We will be raised with Him and we will rest. We celebrate our anticipation of that when we rest and worship one day in seven. There is a day coming when in Jesus we will be at rest forever.

40 THE FRUIT OF LOVE

Q. 60. How is the Sabbath to be sanctified?
A. The Sabbath is to be sanctified by a holy resting all that day, even from such worldly employments and recreations as are lawful on other days; and spending the whole time in the public and private exercises of God's worship, except so much as is to be taken up in the works of necessity and mercy.

> Q. 61. What is forbidden in the fourth commandment?
> A. The fourth commandment forbids the omission or careless performance of the duties required, and the profaning the day by idleness, or doing that which is in itself sinful, or by unnecessary thoughts, words or works, about our worldly employments or recreations.

> Q. 62. What are the reasons annexed to the fourth commandment?
> A. The reasons annexed to the fourth commandment are, God's allowing us six days of the week for our own employments, his challenging a special propriety in the seventh, his own example, and his blessing the Sabbath day.

Perhaps your experience of Sundays is like that described by Laura Ingalls Wilder in her book, *Little House in the Big Woods*:

> On Sundays Mary and Laura must not run or shout or be noisy in their play…. They must sit quietly and listen while Ma read Bible stories to them…. They might look at pictures, and they might hold their rag dolls nicely and talk to them. But there was nothing else they could do.

This had a predictable result for the spirited child Laura. "'I hate Sunday!' she said."[9]

9   Laura Ingalls Wilder, *Little House in the Big Woods* (United States: Harper Collins, 1953), p. 84.

To think of the Sabbath only in terms of what we cannot or must not do robs it of joy, and above all, the Sabbath is to be a joy.[10] The Catechism speaks of 'sanctifying' the Sabbath, that is, of setting it apart. Something set apart is made distinctive from other things. Therefore, it is to be expected that we would live our lives in such a way that Sunday would be different from the rest of our lives. This necessarily means that we will stop doing some things and would do other things. We lose something of the spirit of the day, however, when our emphasis falls upon the restrictions and not upon what those restrictions enable us to do.

The Catechism is quite detailed with regard to what we should and should not do. Some tasks are necessary for life to go on, like preparing dinner ('works of necessity'). Some reflect the gift of mercy to which the day points, like sharing that dinner with others ('works of…mercy'). And all of this is to be suffused with the conscious worship of our redeemer, publicly and privately. We are to cease our ordinary labor and set aside distracting recreations. But the important point here is that *we do so to free ourselves and others for things more necessary.*

Those more necessary things are the things that make us whole. Jesus healed on the Sabbath, and in a sense, the Sabbath exists to heal us. Many things we do, things perfectly good and permissible on other days, should be laid aside one day in seven so that we will learn where our wholeness lies. When we choose to not do something on the Sabbath, we are choosing to open space for better things such as prayer, reading, nurturing friendship, and the like. These are things

10   Isaiah invites us to '… call the Sabbath a delight…' (Isa. 58:13).

for which we often claim to have no time. God gives us the time, if we would obey. To *not* do frees us *to* do. To cease a thing we think we cannot do without forces us to look to Jesus to replace that thing. Looking to Jesus is what the day is about.

There is no joy in mere cessation. No wonder Laura and many after her have learned to 'hate' Sunday. There is joy, however, in genuine worship, in the act of placing our whole spirit, soul, and body into the care of our redeemer God. If letting go of some things one day in seven gets us closer to that joy, then it is wisdom to do so.

Perhaps it might even lead us to say, happily, 'I love Sunday.'

9

How to Love Others

We now begin what some have called the second 'table' of the Law. As the first concerned how we are to love God, this one concerns how we are to love our neighbor.

While the call to love God may at times seem difficult, the call to love others feels impossible. How can we possibly love those we do not like or, harder yet, love those who intend us harm?[1] It helps to know that to love others does not necessarily mean we are to possess warm fuzzy feelings toward them. To love others is to treat them justly and compassionately in the same way we want others to treat us.[2] And *this* is possible.

But it is important to see that in moving from the last chapter to this one, from the first table to the second, we are not really moving at all. Love for others is simply one way by which we show love for God.

When you love my children, you love me. These things cannot be separated. Those amazing people who have loved my kids—school professionals, church members, other

---

1 'But I say to you who hear, Love your enemies, do good to those who hate you…' (Luke 6:27).

2 'You shall love your neighbor as yourself' (Matt. 22:39).

pastors—and have had a significant impact on them have, by extension, touched my heart and honored me. By loving my children, they showed their love for me.

With the second table of the law we actually continue to find ways in which we show love to God, in this case by loving those, and the world, He has made.

41 SHOW HONOR

Q. 63. Which is the fifth commandment?
A. The fifth commandment is,
Honor your father and your mother, that your days may be long in the land that the LORD your God is giving you.

Q. 64. What is required in the fifth commandment?
A. The fifth commandment requires the preserving the honor, and performing the duties, belonging to every one in their several places and relations, as superiors, inferiors or equals.

Q. 65. What is forbidden in the fifth commandment?
A. The fifth commandment forbids the neglecting of, or doing anything against, the honor and duty which belongs to every one in their several places and relations.

> Q. 66. What is the reason annexed to the fifth commandment?
>
> A. The reason annexed to the fifth commandment is a promise of long life and prosperity (as far as it shall serve for God's glory and their own good) to all such as keep this commandment.

My children would often scream one to another, 'You're not the boss of me!' as their definitive rationale for doing what they set out to do without sibling interference. In doing so they were trying to define the authority existing in the relationships of the society in which they were placed. That is, in essence, the importance of the fifth commandment. Though homely in form, speaking of honoring parents, its scope is far broader. It seeks to help us define authority and our response to it. Who is 'the boss' and how do we properly respond?

No society survives without clear lines of authority. Whether we are speaking of the staff at our local grocery, the family in our home, the church we attend, or the country we inhabit, the stability of those organizations depends upon acknowledged roles. The Catechism speaks of these roles as 'superiors,' 'inferiors,' and 'equals.' These terms are not meant to reflect a person's inherent worth but simply the relationships of authority that exist. Some are in a position to command (superiors), others in positions to obey (inferiors), and yet others are peers (equals). In the family, for example, parents are in a superior position to children, and in the workplace employees and their peers are in an inferior position to employers. To carelessly ignore these roles is to destabilize a society. To uphold them is the path, as the Catechism puts it, to 'long life and prosperity.'

Often these roles are well defined and the cost of violating them clear. Failure to perform our duties as an employee leads to the loss of our job. Failure to care for children provokes them to anger. We are to obey rightful authority (when it is handled properly) and those in authority are to lead with care and humility. These matters require wisdom and attention.

The virtue underlying all of this is that of honor. The call is to honor one another in our varying relationships. The house elf Kreacher, in J. K. Rowling's *Harry Potter and the Order of the Phoenix*, was bound to obey the rightful heir of House Black. He did so, but with spite and disdain, and no honor. The commandment calls for honor, not mere obedience.

Restoring honor to our social relationships might do more for the renewal of culture than we might imagine.

This call to nurture the virtue of honor moves in all directions in our social relationships. When Paul tackles the difficult relationships within marriage and family, he reminds all to 'submit to one another out of reverence for Christ.'[3] Both husband and wife, parent and child, are called to submit to one another and so show honor to one another as a way to honor, or reverence, Christ. Whether we lead or follow, we do so honoring others as those created in the image of God.

---

3   Ephesians 5:21.

A friend of mine lost his job a few months ago. When I spoke with him about that he was quite reserved, not wishing to defame his former employers. They may not have deserved his reserve, but he acted with honor toward them because he believed that in so doing he was honoring Christ. He was right.

There are wrongs that must be confronted, sometimes vigorously, but always with honor. There are times when relationships come to an end. A task must be refused, a bond must be broken, a command disobeyed, or injustice confronted. Space forbids teasing out all those situations. But in each case, we must be led by a determination to find some way to honor, as much as we are able, those with whom we are at odds.

Those who wrote the Catechism were at the time of its writing in rebellion against the King of England.[4] This question of 'who is the boss' mattered greatly to men who had just ousted their king. Sometimes a child must break with his parents or a person with his country. But always, always, one must be led to do so in a way that preserves, as much as is possible, the honor of the other, and so, of Christ.

42 UPHOLD LIFE

Q. 67. Which is the sixth commandment?
A. The sixth commandment is,
You shall not murder.

---

4   For details, see the section 'What is the Catechism?'

Q. 68. What is required in the sixth commandment?
A. The sixth commandment requires all lawful endeavors to preserve our own life, and the life of others.

Q. 69. What is forbidden in the sixth commandment?
A. The sixth commandment forbids the taking away of our own life, or the life of our neighbor unjustly, or whatsoever tends thereunto.

The command to not murder seems perfectly straightforward and simple. We should be able to agree that murder is bad and move on.

But it's not so simple.

In fact, the application of this simple command is so broad that all of us have broken it.

Even though the Catechism allows that there are some just occasions for the literal taking of another's life (self-defense, for example), it rightly understands 'murder' to mean anything that tends toward denying life to another. Reckless or drunk driving is a violation of this commandment. Neglecting building codes in such a way that endangers the occupants breaks this commandment. Ignoring opportunities to provide food to the hungry falls under its condemnation. The territory covered by this commandment is strikingly extensive.

Jesus applies this commandment even to angry outbursts.[5] To speak words of venomous hate is, in essence, to wish another dead. Even if we don't actually act on what our words imply, both wish and act tend toward the taking of life and are therefore forbidden. Life is the gift of God and is to be consistently cherished and supported toward friend and enemy alike.

Whenever it lies within our reach to save or preserve or promote the life of another, we are by this commandment required to do so. The unjust taking of a pre-born human life is a violation of this commandment. So too is the denial of asylum to those fleeing life-threatening, drug-war-influenced terror.

At the risk of our own lives and reputations we are to defend the weak. It is a mark of nobility for a man to defend, even to death, the lives and honor of his wife and sons and daughters. It is also noble for us to stand with those violated in some life-altering way by the powerful, such as women sexually abused by their employers or children by their parents. When we accuse the abused of falsehood or mental instability because we fear their powerful abusers, we shrink from our duty and put lives in danger.

Early twenty-first-century America is a violent society. Our superheroes are vigilantes who fight and sometimes kill upon some violation of honor. We consider it right, when pushed, to push back without giving due consideration to

---

5   'You have heard that it was said to those of old, "You shall not murder; and whoever murders will be liable to judgment." But I say to you that everyone who is angry with his brother will be liable to judgment; whoever insults his brother will be liable to the council; and whoever says, "You fool!" will be liable to the hell of fire' (Matt. 5:21-2).

the one who said 'turn the other cheek.'[6] That we celebrate and honor revenge as a right and a necessity suggests we have been nurtured more by our culture than by the teaching of Jesus, the Prince of Peace.

Often the questions that need to be decided are difficult ones. What is the unjust taking of life? What tends in that direction? What might we do to preserve the life of others that we are not now doing? The issues can puzzle us. But perhaps they puzzle us so deeply because we have grown unused to thinking in ways that celebrate life and not violence.

The 1986 movie *The Mission* portrays the deep challenges raised here. Two eighteenth-century priests are moved to find ways to defend their South American tribal congregants against an attacking force intent on enslaving them. One priest chooses to arm his flock and fight the attackers. The other leads his flock simply to hold a cross and pray. We can debate which priest chose rightly, the one who chose peaceful resistance or the one who chose armed.[7] What is not debatable is our too easy tendency to strike out, to scream, to challenge, to seek vengeance, to withhold refuge, to deny food, to do so many things that tend or lead, sadly, to the denial of life to others.

It's not such a simple command after all.

---

6   As said Jesus in Matthew 5:39: 'But I say to you, Do not resist the one who is evil. But if anyone slaps you on the right cheek, turn to him the other also.' There are occasions in which we must defend ourselves. My point here is that we are quick to celebrate violent revenge without giving adequate consideration to what this teaching of Jesus might mean for our situations.

7   A highly relevant debate in churches when more and more places of worship have been violated by armed attackers.

43 PRACTICE CHASTITY

Q. 70. Which is the seventh commandment?
A. The seventh commandment is,
You shall not commit adultery.

Q. 71. What is required in the seventh commandment?
A. The seventh commandment requires the preservation
of our own and our neighbor's chastity, in heart, speech
and behavior.

Q. 72. What is forbidden in the seventh commandment?
A. The seventh commandment forbids all unchaste
thoughts, words and actions.

Many years ago, Barb and I watched a TV mini-series featuring an English ship captain marooned in early sixteenth-century feudal Japan.[8] The captain finds himself attracted to a woman from a Japanese feudal court, and she returns his affection. Though both are married to others, the tension builds over whether they will sleep together. We found ourselves sympathizing with their loneliness and our romantic hearts cheered them on. We cheered them on, that is, to sin. We were hoping (we suddenly realized) that they would break the commandment of God. Our hearts, which

---

8   'Shogun' [https://www.imdb.com/title/tt0080274/]. The point, of course, could be made using any of a thousand other such examples.

have only a very tenuous grasp of this commandment, are easily led astray.

Directly, this seventh commandment teaches that a man is not to have a sexual relationship with a woman (or another man) who is not his wife, and a woman is not to do so with a man (or another woman) who is not her husband. Its intent is clear, but our sentiments plead all kinds of exceptions. The pop song lyric, 'If loving you is wrong, I don't want to be right,'[9] finds resonance in many hearts.

It is not sex that God opposes, as some might suppose. Sex is a beautiful gift of God by which a married couple with physical pleasure and emotional intimacy seals their relationship to one another. They give physical expression to the love, unity, and mutual devotion that is at the heart of the marriage covenant and so deepen their mutual commitment, situating them well to provide a safe and stable place to rear any children God should choose to give them.

Sex is, though, a fragile gift. It is marred when coupled with violence or used to manipulate. When we offer the gift to another outside the clear lines and commitments of marriage, we cheapen that which was intended to seal those commitments. And when an unmarried man and woman sleep together, though both are single, consenting adults, who may claim love for one another, they have misused the gift. They may protest, 'Our sex was protected, and she is taking birth control pills. We enjoyed it. What could be bad about that?' But they have acted unfaithfully. In using sex outside its intended purpose they have misused that which was meant to deepen the bonds within marriage. Physically

---

9   Written by Homer Banks, Carl Hampton, and Raymond Jackson.

they have communicated commitments to another they are unwilling to make publicly or verbally. Sex is cheapened when it is used this way.

There are myriad other ways we sidestep and cheapen this commandment. Some indulge pornography and say that by it they do no harm. Others leer lustfully at the good-looker across the room and believe it to be innocent. We want to know why these things are wrong when they seem to do no harm. And that is our mistake. We want God to explain why these things are wrong, forgetting that it is not necessary for us to understand a commandment to keep it.

The law of God, coming from His loving, wise and holy heart is to be obeyed because it is by definition good and right. To know that any sexual activity outside the constraints of the marriage covenant is displeasing to God should be enough to motivate our obedience. To know that there is a mystical and sacramental nature to the sexual bond should increase our appreciation of the act and our resolve to preserve it for marriage. Our determination to keep this commandment, however, begins at the time when we love and trust Jesus, and not at the point where we finally understand and agree with it.

This beautiful gift of God is not to be cheapened, misused, or defiled even by two lonely strangers in a starlit, feudal Japanese night. Clever screenwriters touch our sentimental hearts and lead us to cheer the lovers so cast together. But God is a much more gracious screenwriter. The blessing we seek will be found in walking in the paths of chastity ordered by His Word.

Many have broken this commandment, even many of you. Please take heart. Forgiveness applies here, too. In the

Gospel of John, Jesus engages a woman clearly guilty of having sex outside of marriage. He drives away those who were her accusers and shows His acceptance of her. Only then does He issue the expected injunction, 'Go and sin no more.'[10] She went away with a reminder of the law she knew, and with a hope she perhaps had not known.

Even in these things, we cannot sin ourselves out of the range of God's love.

44 NURTURE GENEROSITY

> Q. 73. Which is the eighth commandment?
> A. The eighth commandment is,
> You shall not steal.

> Q. 74. What is required in the eighth commandment?
> A. The eighth commandment requires the lawful procuring and furthering the wealth and outward estate of ourselves and others.

> Q. 75. What is forbidden in the eighth commandment?
> A. The eighth commandment forbids whatsoever does or may unjustly hinder our own or our neighbor's wealth or outward estate.

---

10 John 8:11.

On average, Westerners wear an article of clothing seven times before replacing it. Supplying this voracious appetite for cheap clothing is a vast worldwide network of sweatshops in which only two percent of the workers are paid a living wage.[11] Should this matter to the Christian?

The eighth commandment, the Catechism says, forbids our unjustly hindering our neighbor's wealth. Those making our clothes are our neighbors, whether we see them or not. Is it possible that our demand for cheap apparel hinders their ability to survive? If we are among those churning through clothes like hamburgers, are we, by our consumption, stealing from the labor of those already poor? We who pride ourselves that we would never steal as much as a stick of chewing gum might want to consider whether we are guilty of theft nevertheless.

The affluent—and many of us are affluent—are often blind to the sins that affect our possessions. We are blind to the implications of a commandment when that blindness helps us keep our stuff. For generations Christians in the American South justified the owning of men and women who had been stolen from their land. They justified hindering their slaves' wealth to further their own while confessing conformity to the commandments. They could not, or did not want, to see what seems obvious to us now. It is worth asking what our own blindness might be hiding from us.

---

11 From an interview with Dana Thomas, author of *Fashionopolis: The Price of Fast Fashion and the Future of Clothes*, on The Book Review podcast, October 11, 2019. [https://www.nytimes.com/2019/10/11/books/review/podcast-fashionopolis-dana-thomas-beaten-down-worked-up-steven-greenhouse.html]

The Catechism challenges us to see that when we in any way fail to further others' gain, or in some way succeed in hindering it, we have stolen from them. Restaurant servers report that the worst time to be waiting tables is Sunday after the church down the street lets out. Churchgoers, it seems, are lousy tippers. Christians with otherwise squeaky clean rap sheets regularly steal what is due to their neighbors for services provided by failing to leave a just and fair tip on which, in America, a server depends.

Focusing as we too easily do on the 'sins of the flesh' distracts us from the more socially acceptable but equally heinous sins of greed and injustice. Rightfully, churches take issue with things like adultery or homosexuality (concerns of the seventh commandment) and abortion or drunkenness (concerns of the sixth). But we should as well challenge, for example, the executives in our churches who trim services and drive down wages in order to elevate their own earnings and status, a concern of the eighth commandment. We should hold deeply accountable pastors who plead for their followers' contributions, only to then use the money to build multiple homes and to buy jets to flit between them. We cannot allow ourselves to be blind to the ways in which we steal. According to the prophet Malachi, we may not even hesitate to steal from God.[12]

And it is all wrong.

---

12 'Will man rob God? Yet you are robbing me. But you say, "How have we robbed you?" In your tithes and contributions. You are cursed with a curse, for you are robbing me, the whole nation of you. Bring the full tithe into the storehouse, that there may be food in my house' (Mal. 3:8-10a).

It is proper to protect what is our own. It is not wrong to grow our wealth or to be rich. Money is not the evil, but greed, and greed so subtly worms its way into our consciousness.

And greed is suffocated and dies in the presence of the virtue of generosity.

A man once asked Jesus to arbitrate a family estate: 'Teacher, tell my brother to divide the inheritance with me,' he said, no doubt wanting to maximize his take and minimize his brother's.[13] Such thinking we understand. St Augustine once suggested, however, that the Christian's attitude should be expressed in a way like this: 'Master, tell my brother that he may have my inheritance.'[14] Such a generous spirit is often foreign to us. St Augustine, though, may be closer to the heart of Jesus, who reminds this man, '…one's life does not consist in the abundance of his possessions.'[15].

A generous heart cares for a neighbor more than it does for stuff. Our life does not consist in the abundance of our stuff. We should remember this the next time we calculate that tip or decide what clothes to buy and to wear.

---

13 Luke 12:13.

14 The full quote is this: 'He said, "Master, tell my brother to divide the inheritance with me." We say, "Master, tell my brother that he may have my inheritance."' Quoted in Arthur Just, Jr., ed. *Ancient Christian Commentary on Luke* (United States: IVP Academic, 2003).

15 Luke 12:15.

45 Cultivate Honesty

> Q. 76. Which is the ninth commandment?
> A. The ninth commandment is,
> You shall not bear false witness against your neighbor.

> Q. 77. What is required in the ninth commandment?
> A. The ninth commandment requires the maintaining and promoting of truth between man and man, and of our own and our neighbor's good name, especially in witness-bearing.

> Q. 78. What is forbidden in the ninth commandment?
> A. The ninth commandment forbids whatsoever is prejudicial to truth, or injurious to our own or our neighbor's good name.

My summons for jury duty coincided with the start of a murder trial. I was placed in a pool of fifty jurors, from which the attorneys would pick those who would eventually try the case. The stakes were therefore quite high when the defense attorney began the process by looking directly at me.

'Mr Greenwald?'

'Yes, sir.'

'You're a pastor, correct?'

'Yes, sir, I am.'

'Is it ever right to lie?'

The defense intended to argue that the police had used deception in eliciting a confession from the defendant. And so this attorney was looking for jurors who might condemn the police for being loose with the truth. Suddenly, with an entire courtroom staring at me, I had to reflect on the real life application of God's commandments.[16]

To never lie is deeply rooted in American proverbial folklore. Sayings like Benjamin Franklin's 'honesty is the best policy' and George Washington's 'I cannot tell a lie' are reflections of this ninth commandment's tilt toward truth-telling. Even when telling the truth is personally unpleasant ('No, Dad, I did not wash the car like you asked'), our folk wisdom supports the commandment's call to speak truthfully.

However, our folk-wisdom is better than our cultural reality. We are actually very comfortable with falsehood. Disturbingly so. For many, to 'call in sick' when one intends to spend the day at the beach or the pool, is considered normal behavior. To fudge the data on tax forms or a financial statement is winked at. To submit plagiarized research papers or to preach someone else's sermon as one's own is justified. Our culture lures us with a sophisticated disregard for the truth.

As disciples of Christ, we must resist the tug of such things. Churches should never promote their ministries or Christians their causes with deceptive or manipulative imagery or claims (though it happens all the time). Preachers should be ashamed to use skewed data or unverified statistics

---

16 I did not make it through the first round of exclusions ostensibly because I had made the mistake of reading about the trial in the newspaper that morning.

in their sermons, no matter how worthy the aim. Workers should never adjust their time-cards, even in small amounts. Christians should not tilt a story to protect their reputations at the expense of others. The once-popular chorus, 'They'll know we are Christians by our love,' is undermined when Christians are careless with the truth. We love others by giving them truth.

Our commitment to the truth, and to love, should be notable when others' reputations are on the line. We should never be conduits of gossip or falsehood which are, as the Catechism puts it, '…injurious to…our neighbor's good name.' We should be zealous to love our neighbors, and our enemies, by speaking in ways that promote their good name. This is true when speaking privately or publicly, and it is especially true online where rumor and gossip and falsehood spread so easily. We love our neighbors by honoring the truth and by speaking in such a way that guards their reputations.

Are there times when it is okay to lie? Yes. Absolutely. There are those who have no right to the truth, such as those wanting to use it to do harm to another. If I know the whereabouts of an escaped, abused wife or child, I am under no obligation to tell the abuser the location and am in fact justified in misdirection should that be what is necessary to protect the innocent. Careful reflection will open up other areas where wisdom will show that truth should be withheld.

Nevertheless, the whole tilt of our lives should be in the direction of truth. This is what it means to follow Jesus. And perhaps we will change the narrative. Perhaps they'll know we are Christians by our…integrity.

46 EMBRACE CONTENTMENT

Q. 79. *Which is the tenth commandment?*
A. *The tenth commandment is,*
You shall not covet your neighbor's house; you shall not covet your neighbor's wife, or his male servant, or his female servant, or his ox, or his donkey, or anything that is your neighbor's.

Q. 80. *What is required in the tenth commandment?*
A. *The tenth commandment requires full contentment with our own condition, with a right and charitable frame of spirit toward our neighbor, and all that is his.*

Q. 81. *What is forbidden in the tenth commandment?*
A. *The tenth commandment forbids all discontentment with our own estate, envying or grieving at the good of our neighbor, and all inordinate motions and affections to anything that is his.*

A country song can be a snapshot of the human heart. Consider this song released in 2000 by American country singer Sara Evans.

> *Well, the straight haired girls*
> *They all want curls*
> *And the brunettes want to be blonde*
> *It's your typical thing*

It just goes on and on
They say, hey, it's only human
To never be satisfied.[17]

Our daughter, Hannah, blessed with beautiful, curly hair, would spend hours working to straighten it. She was rewarded with this song as her ringtone on Barb's phone. But this could easily be the theme for any of us.

Dissatisfaction with our possessions, our gifts, or our situations can swallow whole any joy we might otherwise have in them. We long for things not ours to have. That is, we covet. As a result of coveting, discontent overwhelms our heart. Dissatisfaction and discontentment, when allowed to fester, breed hurt and damage by the boatload. It is the perceptive observation of the Apostle James that, 'You desire and do not have, so you murder. You covet and cannot obtain, so you fight and quarrel.'[18] It is the covetous heart that lies behind so many more visible sins.

The unfaithful husband does not begin by desiring his neighbor's wife. He begins by allowing discontent to grow in his relationship with his own wife. Instead of seeing her virtues, he begins to note her shortcomings. Discontent with those shortcomings leads to comparison with his neighbor's wife who seemingly lacks those particular shortcomings. Such comparison leads him to covet what he does not have, and that desire unfolds as unfaithfullness.

Discontentment is the root of unhappiness and human division. Engineers, bankers, teachers, athletes, musicians,

---

17   Sara Evans / Tom Shapiro / Tony Martin, ©Sony/ATV Music Publishing LLC, BMG Rights Management.

18   James 4:2.

preachers, writers, mothers, and fathers cannot find joy in their own gifts, accomplishments, abilities, and unique gifted-by-God personalities because they see others they judge to be better. The desire for what others have blinds them to their own unique giftedness. They cannot even celebrate the accomplishments of others because that only intensifies their sense of lack. That which has always been an ugly reality is in our day amplified by social media. We read of another's accomplishments or situation, we magnify them, and we disdain our own. 'My friend's child knows three languages and he's only four! I'm a lousy mother!' It is a common and true saying that 'comparison is the enemy of joy.'

The commandment pleads with us to embrace contentment. But where is contentment found? What aisle in the supermarket stocks it? Where is the link to it on Amazon? Psalm 131 has a beautiful image of the contented person.

> *But I have calmed and quieted my soul,*
> *like a weaned child with its mother;*
> *like a weaned child is my soul within me.*[19]

The weaned child can be held close to its mother's breast without squirming and twisting to be fed. Such a child, knowing she is loved and has a place, can be content and calm. So the Christian is held by the favor of God. Contentment comes when we learn to accept this.

We may reach great heights in our profession and grow wealthy beyond our imaginations. Or we may live life in

---

19   Psalm 131:2.

obscurity, plagued with disability and loss. Either way, the Christian is a weaned child held close to the breast of God. God gives what we need. He will deny us nothing necessary. He will make no mistakes with us. He will not overlook our needs. And when we doubt these things, we are to look to the cross. He has withheld nothing necessary, not even His own son, from us.[20]

That it is 'only human to never be satisfied' is why you and I will never be able to say that we perfectly keep the commandments of God. To covet will be a temptation that is rarely displaced. The only way to displace it is to take our eyes off the thing that attracts and to place our gaze on Jesus. What truly goes on and on is His love and care. We can stop looking for something more, for nothing more is needed.

---

20 'He who did not spare his own Son but gave him up for us all, how will he not also with him graciously give us all things?' (Rom. 8:32).

10

How to Respond to God

When we visit a museum, we go to look, to observe, and to wonder, but not to touch. It is too easy to treat theology in general and the law in particular like a museum. We look at it as a collection of interesting artifacts that are on display out there beyond us but not to be touched by us.

When we go to a gym, however, the greatest folly would be to simply stare and observe. A gym is meant to exercise us, to strengthen us, to benefit us in ways that only come if we engage the tools that are there.

The law is far more like a gym than a museum. It challenges us and engages us. We are meant to touch it and to be touched by it. It points us in a direction and that direction is Jesus. And like a gym, unlike a museum, the benefit only comes with repeated and frequent visits.

To draw out the appropriateness of this analogy is the subject of this next chapter.

47 EQUALLY UNREACHABLE

> Q. 82. Is any man able perfectly to keep the commandments of God?
> A. No mere man since the fall is able in this life perfectly to keep the commandments of God, but does daily break them in thought, word and deed.

'My brother is the complete package,' a friend told me recently. 'He's good looking, he's athletic, he's smart, and he can play anything on the piano.'

I told her, 'I hate perfect people.'

I don't, really. But people who seem to have it all can make us covetous and that makes us uncomfortable. Unless, of course, we are one of the perfect people.

And there is the problem that this answer seeks to explore. There are no perfect people. There are none who keep the commandments perfectly. There are those who *do* believe that they have kept God's commandments flawlessly and that they are unstained by sin. For some this idea of perfection has taken on the character of a settled doctrine of sinlessness. The Catechism, for good reason, judges such claims as mistaken. No mere man (Jesus was not merely a man) has perfectly kept the commandments of God.[1] When Jesus summarizes the commandments as a call to love

---

1   The Catechism here draws a distinction between Jesus, who perfectly kept the law, and the rest of humanity. Jesus was fully man, but not merely so. He was also fully God.

God with all our heart and soul and mind and strength[2] He shows that such perfection is out of reach. We grow in likeness to Christ,[3] yes, but in this life sin will always be present. Perfection is a goal too far removed from reality. It is a summit too high for any to reach.

To claim otherwise requires lowering the summit to make it reachable. If we define obedience to the law as a thing of mere external compliance then we bring it within reach. If, for example, we reduce the demands of the seventh commandment[4] to simply not sleeping with someone else's spouse, or to not dancing, we might be able to pride ourselves in keeping it. But in reducing it we have gutted it. One who keeps such a reduced morality will find himself tolerating, without concern, his impure thoughts of the woman at the Starbucks counter. One who would never cheat on her spouse may refuse to honor and love him. To reduce the law to certain external behaviors makes it seem achievable. Jesus refused such reduction.

My intent here is not to point fingers at other Christians while claiming superiority for myself. (The fact that such finger-pointing is a ready temptation for Christians should be proof enough that perfection is out of reach.) My hope is that we all could accept as true the Catechism's claim that no mere man or woman, no one but Christ, is able or has been able in this life, since the fall, to purify and orient his life to keep the law in all its glory. The reality is that we are

---

2   'And you shall love the Lord your God with all your heart and with all your soul and with all your mind and with all your strength' (Mark 12:30). See also Q/A 41, 42, 'The Definition of Love'.

3   See Q/A 35, 'Those Sanctified'.

4   See Q/A 70-72, 'Practice Chastity'.

far more sinful than we ever could have imagined. We are none of us 'the complete package.'

But this need not lead to despair.

To claim to have no sin is to claim a fiction that diminishes the glory of God in a spectacular way. Imagine a man lost at sea. His ship breaks apart and he clings to a slab of wood and dog-paddles desperately. When he is rescued, still fifteen hundred miles from the nearest shore, he says, 'I was almost there.' With such a claim of achievement, he diminishes the glory of the rescue and in his delusion will not be moved to thank his rescuer. If we are nearly there, if we are drawing close and all that we need is a boost from Jesus for the final lap of our salvation, the glory is ours to claim.

But we are not almost there. We are nowhere close. And to realize this is to shine a light of glory upon our rescuer.

48 Uniquely Unequal

> Q. 83. Are all transgressions of the law equally heinous?
> A. Some sins in themselves, and by reason of several aggravations, are more heinous in the sight of God than others.

On a warm, Florida afternoon I visited with a young family who lived in a rural area near our church. I knocked on the front door of their unique twenty-eight-hundred square-foot log cabin and was immediately and enthusiastically greeted by Tessa, their six-year-old daughter. 'She's been waiting all day for you to come,' said Karyn, Tessa's mother. And as this precious little girl showed me around her house, with special attention paid to the stuffed animals in her room, I was once again reminded of the position I occupy as a pastor in the eyes of God's precious little ones. I was also reminded that when those in my position sin before the eyes of these precious ones, or against them, such sin is 'more heinous in the sight of God than others.' The harm done is incalculable and greater than if the same sin were to have been committed by another.

This is only one way among many by which some sins are rightfully judged as more heinous, more evil, than others.[5]

Some sins are rendered worse than others by the vulnerability of those against whom they are committed. Physical violence against a child or sexual assault against the weak are sins aggravated in character.

To act is worse than the consideration of that act. To lustfully fantasize an affair is sinful. It is clearly worse, though, to act upon that fantasy. We do not trivialize the sinfullness of the thought and the plans that arise from it. But when sinful consideration becomes sinful act, the sin becomes more heinous.

Hypocrisy deepens a sin's evil. As *The Godfather*'s Michael Corleone has his child baptized in the cathedral, his thugs murder a dozen rivals. The murders are bad in their own right, but the evil of it is worsened by the forethought and the timing aimed to correspond with an otherwise holy occasion.

---

5   The *Shorter Catechism*'s big brother, the *Westminster Larger Catechism*, Q/A 151 devotes an entire and very helpful paragraph to detailing what we will only touch upon here.

These distinctions do not minimize the seriousness of any sin. Nevertheless it is necessary to see that there are aggravations which make some sins more odious, more repulsive, and more evil than others.

At the same time we need to be careful we do not create distinctions where none exist. We are tempted to create our own self-justifying value scale. Sins which we or those close to us are not tempted to commit, we elevate on the scale of evil. The sober man, for example, is quick to condemn the drunk. The sins which harm us directly ('You ran that stop light!'), we treat severely. Sins which have no direct impact on us, but harm others deeply ('We don't serve your type here'), we minimize. We need to guard against such self-created scales of severity.

But still, some sins are worse than others, and knowing this should motivate us to take aim particularly at these aggravated and destructive impulses to sin.

And we must remember this: when those to whom we look disappoint us, as they too often do, there is one (no mere man!)[6] to whom we can look who the law perfectly. When others disappoint, we can still look to Him knowing He will never fail us.

49 EQUALLY CONDEMNED

> Q. 84. What doth every sin deserve?
> A. Every sin deserves God's wrath and curse, both in this life, and that which is to come.

---

6   On the term 'mere man' see footnote 1 on p. 182.

A classic Calvin and Hobbes comic strip shows Calvin's long-suffering mother meticulously readying herself for a formal outing.[7] She dresses, puts on earrings and makeup, and contentedly opens the front door, only to be met by a laughing six-year-old Calvin who sprays her with a garden hose. In the final frame Calvin is grumbling, 'Boy. What a grouch.' Because he does not see his act in the way that she sees it, and as we see it, he does not understand her anger. He can only judge her as being too prickly, which is the way some of us judge God.

Some look at this claim of the Catechism that 'every sin deserves God's wrath and curse' with deep skepticism. The word 'every' is the offending one. True, they acknowledge, there is sin that is worthy of some kind of judgment. But they judge that their sin, such as it is, does not rise to that level. Unable or unwilling to see their sin in the way that God sees it leaves them unable to understand how He could be so upset. They judge Him as being unworthy of anger, and in so doing they fail to see how greatly they are in need of His mercy.[8]

Sin, all of it, is by its definition a refusal to bow before the authority of our rightful King. Each and every sin is a declaration of independence from our Creator and the

---

7   http://www.gocomics.com/calvinandhobbes/2019/06/12, accessed 10/18/19.

8   I am painfully aware of the vast number of sensitive people who are disposed to see their sin all too clearly and to bear that weight with deep anguish. While needing to persuade the cavalier of their danger, I don't want to make the experience of the sensitive worse. The goal for both is the same: to see the wonder and the richness of the mercy of God in Christ.

embracing of a rival lord. By each sin we claim to know better than God about what is right for us to do. Each sin is an affront to the absolute and glorious holiness of God. To minimize the impact of even the smallest (to us!) of sins requires us to dial back our sense of the holy character and perfection of God. Sin is ultimately a theological decision denying the majesty of the one true God. As sin, any sin, aims us toward something other than God, it turns us toward a false god. Sin is far worse, therefore, than we judge it to be. The Apostle Paul echoes David's theology in saying that among people '…no one does good, not even one…'[9] and concludes that '…all have sinned and fall short of the glory of God….'[10]

As we have already seen, some sins are clearly more heinous than others. We have no problems allowing the wrath and curse of God to apply to the crimes of Hitler or to the purveyor of child pornography. To see that the same wrath and judgment falls on us is a harder pill to swallow. *Every* sin deserves God's proper judgment in this life and the next. Every rebellious thought, every angry word, every sarcastic put down, every refusal to help those in need is an affront to the perfect holiness of God. If we could see the nature of our sin from the perspective of a holy God we would not question the propriety of His judgment.

We should in fact be thankful for the just judgment of a holy God. Wickedness that seems to go unpunished in this life will meet its proper fate in the life which is to come. This is not karma, which is impersonal. This is the judgment of the living and true, the personal, infinite, and holy God.

9   Romans 3:12; see also Psalm 14:1.
10   Romans 3:23.

This judgment is deeper and far worse than any notion of karma.

But where does that leave us? It should leave us in great fear and desperate to find an escape. That there is an escape, and one that comes from this same true and holy God, has been the message of the Catechism from the beginning. This holy God freely provides a redeemer. A high view of sin does not reveal God to be a prickly grouch. It reveals Him to be full of mercy beyond measure. In the end a Christian is not merely a sinner saved. He is one beloved, who has been rescued from the wrath and curse of God.

50 THE ESCAPE

> Q. 85. What does God require of us that we may escape his wrath and curse due to us for sin?
> A. To escape the wrath and curse of God due to us for sin, God requires of us faith in Jesus Christ, repentance unto life, with the diligent use of all the outward means whereby Christ communicates to us the benefits of redemption.

Our son, Colin, Barb, and I were hiking a trail on the southernmost tip of the island of Hawaii. Though spread out far enough that we could not see each other, we were confident that each knew the way so none of us worried. We walked silently, engrossed in the remote beauty of the place. Colin was so engrossed that he missed the turn that led to our car. The maze of paths led him deep into the wilderness scrub before he became aware that he was lost. Night was falling, and when he realized that he was lost (though he may not have been aware of his genuine danger), he was overwhelmed, disoriented, and desperate.

The Catechism exposes the engrossing beauty of the person of God and the wonder of His ways. But it also alerts us to our lostness in the face of a rapidly approaching night. It summarizes for us the high expectations of the holy God[11] and lays those expectations on all. There are none who do not sin.[12] Though some sins are more heinous than others[13] no sin, no matter how seemingly inconsequential to us, escapes the judgment of God.[14]

This brew has a bitter, terrible taste. And yet, when we drink these truths deeply, we find mercy. For only when we are persuaded of our lostness will we seek a way out and accept a rescue before night falls.

That there is a way out the Catechism has established in its discussion of Christ as our redeemer.[15] God has provided for our otherwise impossible rescue through His Son. The way out of our lostness for those whom God has effectually called is to 'embrace Jesus Christ.'[16]

That is all, and there lies the true wonder of Christianity. To find our rescue, we need perform no heroic works. No demand is made that we atone for past sins. It is Christ

---

11   In the commandments, Q/A 45-81.

12   Q/A 82.

13   Q/A 83.

14   Q/A 84.

15   See Chapter Four, 'The Provision of a Redeemer.'

16   Q/A 31.

who has provided the atonement and done the works. It remains for us only and solely to embrace Jesus Christ. The Catechism teaches here that 'embracing' Him is a step of faith and repentance, practiced through gracious means that bring our sinful hearts into union with the pure and righteous Christ. Don't be troubled that you don't quite yet understand what all this means. In what follows, the Catechism explains all of this. The point here is simply this: to those who are lost, no matter how far they have strayed, and no matter how deeply they comprehend their danger, in Christ there is escape. There is a way out.

Colin found a lone person in the desolate waste of his lostness. This person pointed to a distant windmill farm and told him to stop going the way he was going and to walk toward the windmills. In trusting this redirection, he was reunited with his trembling parents and escaped his life-threatening danger just as the sun set over the Pacific. This is all that God requires of us. We are to trust the Gospel's redirection. We turn our backs on the way we are going and aim toward Jesus. In that direction, and in that alone, lies the escape we seek, the rescue we need.

51 FAITH

Q. 86. What is faith in Jesus Christ?
A. Faith in Jesus Christ is a saving grace, whereby we receive and rest upon him alone for salvation, as he is offered to us in the gospel.

Once, a conversation among my teenaged friends turned to religion. One said something like this: 'To be a Christian you need to believe that Jesus died on the cross for your sins and to trust in Him to save you from God's judgment.' He said this without passion and without personal commitment. He had the same knowledge as I, but I was a Christian, and my friend was not. We were two people accessing the same belief content and yet only one could be said to have faith. The faith that saves is therefore clearly more than the possession of certain facts. But what is it?

A similar, but considerably more sophisticated and more public discussion occurred between *New York Times* columnist Nicholas Kristof and New York City pastor Tim Keller.[17] Again, here were two people accessing the same belief content with only one, Keller, responding with faith. Kristof clearly appreciates what he understands about Christianity, but he denies being a Christian. He knows Christian things but does not possess Christian faith. The faith that saves moves beyond one's intellectual and emotional engagement with Christianity to engage the will. Saving faith is an act of the will by which one 'receive[s] and rests' upon Jesus for salvation.

A way to understand this is to consider another conversation, this time between two dying men.[18] Jesus was crucified between two convicted criminals. One of the two spoke boldly of Jesus, speaking of His power and

---

17 'Am I a Christian, Pastor Timothy Keller?' by Nicholas Kristof, December 23, 2016, https://nyti.ms/2imuM3J (accessed 10/18/19).

18 You can read the entire conversation in Luke 23.

even confessing that Jesus had the power to save them from death.[19] Based on this knowledge he demanded of Jesus, 'Save us!' It is clear that he was only seeking to be saved from his crucifixion. The only danger he saw was the blood leaking from his hands, and the only role he would accept for Jesus was that of a powerful wonder worker who could get him out of his jam. There is faith here, but it is not saving faith.

The other criminal, too, had knowledge of Jesus' teaching and power. He, however, was moved by something deeper.[20] He was aware that he and the other were dying for crimes that they had committed. He knew they had no right to ask to be delivered from the judgment due to them for their guilt before people. But he sensed a deeper need. He saw that Jesus was innocent and that Jesus' kingdom, and therefore His purposes, were not centered in the matters of this world. His request of Jesus, his prayer, is a humble acknowledgment that only Jesus could save him from his guilt before God. By his prayer he rested his hope on Jesus alone for his salvation. The salvation he sought was more than rescue from the immediacy of death. He sought rescue from divine judgment and believed that Jesus could provide it. He wanted more than mere life. He wanted life with God.

The men had similar knowledge of Jesus but a different understanding of their own need. One appealed to Christ's

---

19 'One of the criminals who were hanged railed at him, saying, "Are you not the Christ? Save yourself and us!"' (Luke 23:39).

20 'But the other rebuked him, saying, "Do you not fear God, since you are under the same sentence of condemnation? And we indeed justly, for we are receiving the due reward of our deeds; but this man has done nothing wrong." And he said, "Jesus, remember me when you come into your kingdom"' (Luke 23:40-2).

power out of self-interest. The other appealed to Christ's mercy out of desperation. There is the difference. When we come to see the depth of our sin we cannot appeal to our goodness, and we have no right to demand anything from the power of God. All that we can do is to throw ourselves upon the mercy of God in Jesus and ask Him to remember us and to save us.

That is the faith that brings us into a saving relationship with a savior. Though we call this 'saving faith,' the faith itself does not save. Faith, rather, is the act by which we surrender to the salvation that Jesus provides. The line dividing the one who has faith and the one who does not runs not through the intellect but through the will.[21] It is pride and fear that sometimes keeps those who know the truth from surrendering to Jesus and all that that might mean. Saving faith is an act, often courageous and bold, of the will.

Those who do surrender to Him, who receive and rest upon Him alone, eventually come to see something remarkable and humbling. They see that it is God who gives the gift of that faith.[22] It is God who moves the will. Faith is not just an act. It is, as the Catechism says, a saving *grace*. It is a grace we pray for and desire for all, from high school friends to famous columnists. And it is a grace that, when we see it in ourselves, moves us not to pride but to deep gratitude.

---

21 This is why the Catechism includes the renewal of the will as one of the elements of effectual calling (Q/A 31).

22 'For by grace you have been saved through faith. And this is not your own doing; it is the gift of God' (Eph. 2:8).

52 Repentance

> Q. 87. What is repentance unto life?
> A. Repentance unto life is a saving grace, whereby a sinner, out of a true sense of his sin, and apprehension of the mercy of God in Christ, does, with grief and hatred of his sin, turn from it unto God, with full purpose of, and endeavor after, new obedience.

When Dorothy from Kansas finds herself traveling through the strange and wonder-filled land of Oz, she encounters a fork in the yellow brick road.[23] This puzzles her, of course. How could she follow the yellow brick road, as the Munchkins had advised, and so return to Kansas, if that road goes in two different directions?

Dorothy's dilemma mirrors that of the person who becomes a Christian. Many ways to live as a Christian are offered to him, and all seem viable. Those who embrace the Christian faith infer that there must be a change of life associated with that faith, but what does that look like? Jesus says, 'Repent and believe in the gospel.'[24] But what is this thing called repentance? It can feel confusing.

So, what is repentance?

Repentance, like faith, is an act of the will. It is a turning from something to something else. It is an act that changes us. It is not nothing. It is the choice to follow Jesus, to set out on the road that leads to life and to abandon the road

---

23 These allusions refer to the 1939 movie, *The Wizard of Oz*.

24 Mark 1:15.

that leads to death. And like faith, it is an act of the will that is made at the point we first come to Christ, and it is the defining orientation of our lives thereafter.

And yet we must say that repentance is not sinlessness, and it is not perfection. It is not merely a change of mind, though it is that, and it is not merely changed behavior, though it is that, too. It is the orientation of our lives, guided by faith, to be a follower of Jesus.

Certainly, some Christians appear to be better at following Jesus than others. Some make great strides in their new obedience while others often stumble and fall. Some see great progress and others only failure. Some set out following Him faithfully only to be overwhelmed repeatedly by old temptations and weaknesses.

Presuming that repentance must be visible and measurable, we ask, 'How much repentance is enough?' But repentance as an act of the will and an orientation of the heart may not always be easily seen or measured.

Our fear is that God expects a certain level of accomplishment from our repentance and that we are not achieving it. That concern is misplaced. We need to remember that our salvation is secured by Jesus, not by us. Salvation is a result of union with Him, not a result of our ability to amass a certain level of heroic Christian deeds. As well, we need to realize that repentance, like faith, is not measured but placed. Faith can be strong or weak, but as it reaches out to Jesus it is enough. So, too, repentance can be vigorous or faltering, but as it is aimed toward Jesus, it is sufficient. The question is not one of measuring success but assessing direction. And repentance is the heart aimed toward following Jesus.

Repentance is more this orientation of the heart to follow after Jesus than it is actual success in that following. We expect to see some measure of outward conformity in the Christian, but the outward achievement is not repentance. Otherwise it can be too easily counterfeited. A child can choose to be obedient because he fears being beaten, or he can obey because he loves his parents. Christian repentance is more similar to the latter. It flows from an understanding of God's mercy out of which we learn to hate our sin and desire to turn from it. Repentance is an orientation of the heart before it is an observable act.

We aim toward obedience, but when we fail, our eternal destiny is not thrown into question. Rather, when we fail, we are to once again remember the mercy of God. We are to grieve our sin as an offense against our Father, the holy God who saved us. In that light, we hate our sin. And in hatred of the sin, steeped in the mercy of our Father, we turn from it, renewed again with the desire to follow Him. Repentance, therefore, is a part of the Christian's daily life and a key weapon against the dominance of sin.

When Dorothy is confronted with multiple directions, she is met by the (brainless!) Scarecrow who directs her in both directions simultaneously. In this he is not a good guide. There are not multiple ways to go. In only one way is the mercy of God to be found.

11

Living in the Way of Grace

Walking along the outside deck of a cruise ship on the Mediterranean Sea, Barb and I came upon a part of the walkway that was made of glass. Here we were given an unobstructed view of the waters beneath. Barb walked unhesitatingly forward, entrusting the full weight of her body and her life to Holland American Cruise Lines and its engineers. I hesitated. Reason told me that the cruise company would take no unnecessary risks with the lives of its paying customers. But my body rebelled at the idea of standing over The-Sea-That-Swallowed-Jonah with no visible means of support. I eventually stepped forward but not without some uncertainty.

Barb had strong faith, leading to boldness. Mine was weak, leading to timidity. And what was true that day is reversed other days.

Just like in the church.

There we find some Christians whose faith is strong and alive, and we find others who struggle to believe and find every step of obedience a labor.

God knows this. And out of His kindness He has given to us what are called the 'means of grace' so that our faith might be nurtured and strengthened. We will discuss these in the pages that follow. The invitation is for us to place ourselves in those places where God reveals His grace, His kindness, and His favor so that there He might strengthen us and deepen our trust in Him.

As we live in this way of grace, we might find not only the courage to step freely onto the glass, but as well the joy of dancing there.

53 THIN PLACES

> Q. 88. What are the outward and ordinary means whereby Christ communicates to us the benefits of redemption?
> A. The outward and ordinary means whereby Christ communicates to us the benefits of redemption, are his ordinances, especially the Word, sacraments, and prayer; all which are made effectual to the elect for salvation.

A hymn Christians sing has this line:

> *Prone to wander, Lord I feel it*
> *prone to leave the God I love.*[1]

Though this sentiment resonates with many Christians it seems irrational. Given all that we have learned thus far of

---

1   Robert Robinson, 'Come, Thou Fount of Every Blessing', *The Trinity Hymnal, Revised Edition*, #457.

God's greatness, His mercy, His work of kindness on the cross, and His power in the resurrection, why would anyone leave such a God or neglect such a great salvation? It makes no sense until we remember that we are children. Christians wander because we are children.

When Seth, our son, was two, our family ventured into a crowded McDonald's then operating on a boat moored on the Mississippi River at the foot of St Louis' famous Gateway Arch.[2] Barb and I, with my parents and our daughter, were looking for seats when we realized that Seth was missing. After a quick and frantic search we found him on the gangway trying with all his effort to get above the rail to look at the water beneath. It was not smart, but he was a child. Children wander when they forget the dangers around them and the benefits of being close to those who love them and can protect them.

Christians, like children, wander when they forget the dangers of life and neglect the benefits of being close to the God who loves them and can protect them. Knowing the volatility of faith and its need to be nurtured and strengthened and fed, God has given Christians means by which we may be nurtured in our faith and kept close to Him. We have come to call these practices the 'means of grace.' These visible ('outward') and unspectacular ('ordinary') practices of the Word, the sacraments,[3] and prayer, are the means that God's Spirit uses to care for and

---

2   I found the placement of a restaurant famous for its 'golden arches' just beneath the country's most famous arch to be humorous. Whether it was meant to be or not I cannot say. Sadly, it no longer exists.

3   That is, baptism and the Lord's Supper.

encourage His people. Some find it helpful to think of these as 'thin' places where proximity to God may seem more real and where Christians can more easily see and trust the benefits of Christ. The Spirit's work is often invisible and is rarely dramatic, but through regular engagement with the ordinary means of grace the Christian's often unsteady faith is fed and strengthened so that, in the end, it will not fail.

None of these means are magic, and none of them are instant fixes for the struggling Christian. A single meal seems to have little impact on a body's overall health, but regular eating is necessary for the sustaining of life. So, too, we may find little immediate impact from a single sermon or isolated trip to the communion table. But a lifestyle of participation will find us who are prone to wander, safely and joyfully in the presence of God at the end. These thin places are the means by which God, through His Spirit, has chosen to minister His grace to His people. They are God's gifts to us for our strengthening.

An examination of each of these means of grace will now occupy us. Seeing how important these things are in themselves will, as well, feed our desire for public worship where these means are primarily provided. My goal is to encourage us in the use of the means of grace, that we would all be able to live our lives in the joy of knowing that God will hold His children close. Yes, we are prone to wander. But by the means of grace God takes our hands and holds His children close.

54 GOD'S WRITTEN WORD

> Q. 89. How is the Word made effectual to salvation?
> A. The Spirit of God makes the reading, but especially the preaching, of the Word, an effectual means of convincing and converting sinners, and of building them up in holiness and comfort, through faith, unto salvation.

> Q. 90. How is the Word to be read and heard, that it may become effectual to salvation?
> A. That the Word may become effectual to salvation, we must attend thereunto with diligence, preparation and prayer; receive it with faith and love, lay it up in our hearts, and practice it in our lives.

Our Australian Shepherd, Addie, knew the place to be if she were to get to eat something other than dry dog food. During our dinner she would place herself on the floor either near or under the table. When our children were young, she ate often. When they were older, she did not always score a snack. Nevertheless, knowing that this was the place where snacks would occur, she regularly and faithfully put herself, we might say, in the way of treats.

Sometimes people lament that they read their Bibles or attend church or hear sermons and 'get nothing out of it.' I understand this. I'm no different. But it does not follow that such activities are useless. Wise Christians place themselves where the gifts of God are dispensed by the Spirit of God.

They will put themselves in the way of grace. Sometimes the grace received will be rich and other times it will seem sparing. Nevertheless, like our Addie, hungry for blessing, we place ourselves where we know blessing is to be found.

One such place of grace is where the Scriptures are read and faithfully preached. It is there that God builds up His people in holiness while comforting, guiding, and supporting them in their Christian walk. To attend public worship, especially, hungry to hear God, not just to fulfill a duty, is to place oneself in the way of grace. How can we do this in a way that prepares us to receive the greatest blessing? The Catechism directs us in several ways.

First, we are to attend with 'diligence, preparation, and prayer.' Not only are we to be faithful in attendance, but we are to prepare for worship before we arrive. We are to pray that our hearts would be ready to hear and that those preaching would preach with faithfullness to Scripture, with honesty and with power.

Secondly, we are to attend, ready to receive the Word 'with faith and love.' We come ready to hear God, not to criticize the preacher. When Scripture is preached, God speaks and thus there is value. Not every preacher is a gifted orator, and not every preacher will be 'on' every week. Nevertheless, as every faithful and able preacher presents Scripture, we are to be ready to receive it as God's Word for us.

Thirdly, we are to 'lay [Scripture] up in our hearts.' We memorize it when we are able. But always we take what is read and spoken and reflect on it. It is not wise to let it slip through our fingers. Discuss it with others if possible. Write a journal entry if you can. Receive the Word with thoughtful care.

Finally, we are to 'practice it.' As much as we are able, we are to act upon what we hear.

All that is said here regarding our public engagement with the Word applies equally to our private reading as well. In both cases, Scripture is a means of grace.

And yet, we can never force the work of the Holy Spirit. Even after we have done everything, we will sometimes return home from hearing the Word preached or raise our eyes from the written page, and will have hearts that are still cold and unmoved. But the Spirit is working, and the Word of God always has power, even when it seems that nothing is happening. Not every meal is spiced with delight, but every meal served from the Scriptures nourishes a soul that has no other food.

The Spirit works without pomp and spectacle, through ordinary and faithful preachers who preach Scripture from the heart out of love for God and for God's people. There is power there. Put yourselves in the way of this grace.

55 God's Visible Word

Q. 91. How do the sacraments become effectual means of salvation?

A. The sacraments become effectual means of salvation, not from any virtue in them, or in him that does administer them; but only by the blessing of Christ, and the working of his Spirit in them that by faith receive them.

Q. 92. What is a sacrament?

A. A sacrament is an holy ordinance instituted by Christ; wherein, by sensible signs, Christ, and the benefits of the new covenant, are represented, sealed, and applied to believers.

Q. 93. Which are the sacraments of the New Testament?

A. The sacraments of the New Testament are baptism and the Lord's Supper.

When Jerusha, our youngest daughter, was fifteen, she and I would meet every two weeks at a coffee shop for conversation and a game of chess. She would drink coffee of some variety and I would sip hot chocolate or tea. I was fifty but had never drunk coffee, to Jerusha's great consternation. So we made an agreement: if she were to beat me in a game of chess before I turned fifty-one, I would drink a cup of coffee.[4] We set the terms of our wager and wrote them on the back of a Panera receipt. Then we each signed it to seal our commitment to those terms.

God's covenant, of which we have spoken before,[5] is the way in which God has chosen to establish a relationship with His people. The covenant is not a wager, of course, but it is an arrangement in which the parties involved pledge

---

4   That, as I write, there is a cup of coffee at my side is a hint as to how this particular arrangement played out.

5   See particularly Chapter Three, 'The Brokenness of Creation' and the section, 'The Covenant Set.'

themselves to certain obligations. God, in establishing the covenant with His people, provides certain visible means, symbols, by which the terms of the covenant might be remembered, and by which the parties involved seal their commitment.

Like signatures on the back of a Panera receipt.

What we know of as the sacraments of baptism and the Lord's Supper are such symbols and seals. These are two rites, or practices of the church, by which God's invisible promises are represented to His people, and by which God seals His pledge to be faithful to these promises. By our participation in the sacraments we, by faith, receive the blessing of Christ in the covenant and pledge to walk faithfully in all that this covenant entails. The sacraments are signs by which the invisible promises of God are made visible. By them God's people are reminded of the pledge of God to be faithful to His promises. As preaching conveys God's Word in a spoken fashion, the sacraments make His Word visible and tangible.

The sacraments are more than ceremonies with theological content. They have a real effect upon the participant. The benefits of our redemption flowing from God's covenant are, in the sacraments, applied by the Spirit to those who receive them in faith. This has a true and necessary impact on the recipient's heart and faith. They bring visually, in outward form, and inwardly, by the Spirit's work, the reality that God has sealed His promises to us, that He has signed the pledge, and that He has agreed to the deal. As He has promised with the blood of His Son and the gift of His Spirit to be a God to us and to our children, the sacraments are a reminder that He will never hesitate to be faithful to these promises.

We need such reminders, as I have already said many times, because we so easily forget.

And when we forget, our faith burns low. Preaching reminds us of the promises, and the sacraments are God's seal upon those promises. They are God's Word made visible to remind the struggling Christian that though he may be prone to wander, God is not.

Christian, you need the sacraments, not merely to show the world the reality of your faith but to take in a fresh way to yourself the certainty of the promises of God.

God seals, and keeps, His Word. We need to see that and experience it. We do so in the sacraments.

56 THE SIGN OF BELONGING

> Q. 94. What is baptism?
> A. Baptism is a sacrament, wherein the washing with water in the name of the Father, and of the Son, and of the Holy Ghost, does signify and seal our ingrafting into Christ, and partaking of the benefits of the covenant of grace, and our engagement to be the Lord's.

> Q. 95. To whom is baptism to be administered?
> A. Baptism is not to be administered to any that are out of the visible church, till they profess their faith in Christ, and obedience to him; but the infants of such as are members of the visible church are to be baptized.

A young woman in our church on her first attendance at a worship service after accepting her fiancé's proposal wore her new ring like a crown. This symbol said something, something she had desired for a good portion of her life. It proclaimed to any who saw it, but especially to the bearer, that she was the object of another's special affection. The ring was a marker of a committed and precious relationship which would have no end.

The sacrament of baptism is such a marker.

Baptism, a symbolic cleansing with water, marks the recipient as bearing a special and precious relationship with God. It is thus a seal upon God's promises to him and a mark of the Christian's inclusion as a part of God's covenant people.

Baptism is practiced differently in different branches of the Christian church. Some churches completely immerse the recipient in water and some sprinkle or pour the water. The distinctions are important but beyond our ability to address here. It is enough to say that the power of the sacrament lies in its substance and not in its mode of application.

Some believers view baptism as an act by which they make a statement about themselves. By this act they profess their faith in and commitment to God. Though this is a part of what goes on in baptism, baptism's primary significance lies not in what we do, but in what God is doing. In baptism God reaffirms His promises to the sinner in need of grace. As those baptized bear the stain of sin, baptism signifies God's removal of that stain. As those baptized come as wayward sheep, by baptism God brands them as His own. Baptism is not primarily something we do, but something God does. In baptism God publicly affirms His pledge to be our God and claims us as His people.

Thus, baptism is no empty ritual but an important marker of a Christian's standing with God. When Christians question their salvation they often look inside themselves for signs of salvation. There is value in this, but we must not overlook the sign that God Himself has given as a marker of our salvation. Baptism is meant to signify God's favor to us. We need to accept it as such.

Of course, all signs can be misused. A woman can put on an engagement ring solely to keep unwanted suitors away or a man can remove his wedding band to hide his infidelity. But the proper use of a sign is to see it pointing to something we might sometimes question. Your baptism is meant to hold you close to Jesus, to remind you that even with your weak faith, the promises of God are strong. You are engaged to be His, and He does not back away from His promises.

All Christians believe that this sign of inclusion in the covenant community belongs to those who profess faith. The Catechism teaches that it belongs as well to the children of believers. Throughout the Bible, God's covenants have applied to the children of those who embrace those covenants. The sign of covenant inclusion in the Old Testament, circumcision, was commanded to be given to the children of covenant members. There is no persuasive reason to think that this grace of inclusion, now marked by baptism, would be withdrawn from children. The children of believers, by virtue of this covenant relationship, are rightful heirs of the covenant, and as such have a right to wear the sign of the covenant. All that this might mean and not mean we cannot address here. Nevertheless, that the children of the covenant are meant to enjoy the sign of inclusion is—the Catechism teaches—an important implication of the covenant.

My newly engaged friend looked often at her ring finger as a way of 'pinching' herself into a reminder of her happy, new reality. We who follow Christ should also look often with happiness and comfort to our baptism. It reminds us of whose we are and always will be.

57 THE SIGN OF LIFE

> Q. 96. What is the Lord's Supper?
> A. The Lord's Supper is a sacrament, wherein, by giving and receiving bread and wine according to Christ's appointment, his death is showed forth; and the worthy receivers are, not after a corporal and carnal manner, but by faith, made partakers of his body and blood, with all his benefits, to their spiritual nourishment and growth in grace.

> Q. 97. What is required to the worthy receiving of the Lord's Supper?
> A. It is required of them that would worthily partake of the Lord's Supper, that they examine themselves of their knowledge to discern the Lord's body, of their faith to feed upon him, of their repentance, love, and new obedience; lest, coming unworthily, they eat and drink judgment to themselves.

In fifty-seven words the Catechism cuts through millennia of discussion, controversy, and (at times, sadly) bloodshed regarding the nature and place of the Lord's Supper in the life of the Christian church. The Catechism draws our attention to the Supper's clear symbolism as a visible rite whereby, using bread and wine,[6] Christ's death is displayed and called to the Christian's remembrance. The Catechism, as well, draws our attention to the sacrament's essential significance and power.

When Christians eat the bread and drink the wine (symbols which remain bread and wine) they become one with them in the clearest way possible. In so doing they are by faith taking to themselves the body and blood of Jesus, portraying and embracing their union, their oneness, with Him. A Christian's eternal destiny is secured through union with Christ, and this sacrament portrays that union as starkly as possible.[7] The act of receiving the bread and drinking the wine does not re-enact the events of Calvary and the empty tomb, nor does it merely remind us of these events. At the table our union with Christ in His death and resurrection is celebrated and our relationship with Him renewed. By this rite we are graciously kept close to Jesus, and by this table we come time and again to receive nourishment from Him to enable us to press on in our Christian lives. At the table Christ Himself nurtures and strengthens our often precarious faith.

---

6   I speak of wine here not to delegitimize the practice of using grape juice, common to many churches, but to acknowledge both my preference as well as the Catechism's own language.

7   The sacrament itself is not what saves.

And this is no simple table.[8] Certainly around it gather those whom we can see in the congregation with whom we physically partake. But, as well, around the table are seated all the Christians in all the world and all the Christians who have ever lived. This is the table of the family of God gathered to feast with and on Jesus. *Together* we take the bread and we take the wine and are reminded that the benefits we have in Him unite us with a vast company. Christians of every tribe and language gather here, as well as the rich and the poor. We sit at this table beside saints and martyrs. It is a privileged place we share.

Not everyone, though, has rightful access to the Lord's Supper.[9] Just as we can't simply walk into anyone's house, sit down, and expect to be fed, so too there are boundaries to be honored in this supper. Clearly, since this is a covenant meal, those who take part should be professing believers who are marked by baptism as being covenant members.

Covenant membership is required. Spiritual perfection is not. In fact, those most aware of their imperfections are those who will often most benefit by the Supper's gracious strengthening. The table encourages us to examine ourselves and our relationship to God and to others in the light of the grace of God. Where there is division, we seek to be reconciled. Where there is sin, we seek the grace of repentance. In the act of coming to the table we express our longing to be more like Christ.

---

8   To speak of communion as a 'table' is to speak of its nature as a meal around which Christians gather. We acknowledge that most Christians do not, in taking communion, sit around a literal table.

9   This sacrament has several names. As the 'Lord's Supper' it is the meal by which we are fed by Christ. As the 'eucharist' it is an act of thanksgiving for the mercy shown to us in Christ. As 'communion' we share a meal not only with Jesus the host but with the whole body of Christ.

Christians consistently find themselves letting go of Jesus to take hold of lesser things. In light of our weakness, God has given us this sacrament to call us back to Him. In it we turn away from false dependencies and once again take hold of Jesus, acknowledging with powerful imagery that we need Him, and that apart from Him we cannot survive. This sacrament is, along with the Word preached, a very real vehicle by which God communicates His grace to us. It is thus regularly (I believe as frequently as we are able) to be a part of Christian worship. And Christians, needy as we are, should not willfully keep themselves from it.

58 THE POWER OF GRACE

> Q. 89. How is the word made effectual to salvation?
> A. The Spirit of God makes the reading, but especially the preaching, of the word, an effectual means of convincing and converting sinners, and of building them up in holiness and comfort, through faith, unto salvation.

> Q. 91. How do the sacraments become effectual means of salvation?
> A. The sacraments become effectual means of salvation, not from any virtue in them, or in him that does administer them; but only by the blessing of Christ, and the working of his Spirit in them that by faith receive them.

Some have criticized the Catechism because it lacks a specific presentation of the person and work of the Holy Spirit. It is true that there are no questions and answers addressing the Holy Spirit directly. It is not true that the Catechism takes inadequate notice of the Spirit.

The Holy Spirit is, we are told, God, infinite, eternal, and unchangeable.[10] He is a person of the Trinity equal in power and glory with the Father and the Son.[11] Through Him the Son reveals to us the will of God for our salvation[12] and it is by Him that that salvation is applied to the elect.[13] And, as the answers to the two questions here revisited remind us, it is the Holy Spirit who works in and through the means of grace to unite us to Christ and to effect holiness and blessing in us. The Holy Spirit is everywhere in the Catechism as He is everywhere in the life of the Christian.

Even with all of this, though, we only scratch the surface of what could be said about the Holy Spirit.[14] The Holy Spirit works to bring us into faith and understanding, and He works to hold us there. When the Scriptures come alive for us, it is because the Holy Spirit has shed light upon them.[15] When our hearts are overwhelmed with the reality of our sin in a way that leads to a deep desire for repentance

---

10   Q/A 4.

11   Q/A 6.

12   Q/A 24.

13   Q/A 29-31.

14   Worth a visit is the work of John Owen, a seventeenth-century Puritan, whose writing on the Holy Spirit is eye-opening and mind-blowing: *The Works of John Owen*, Volumes 3 and 4 (United States: The Banner of Truth Trust, 1966, 1967).

15   See John 16:13; 1 Corinthians 2:14. It should be said that so rich is the New Testament teaching on the Holy Spirit that it is difficult

and a desire to walk in a way pleasing to Christ, that is the work of the Holy Spirit.[16] When there are occasions where we simply do not know how or what to pray—when, perhaps, overcome with grief or fear or confusion—the Holy Spirit comes alongside of us to pray with and for us in ways that we cannot understand.[17] He is the one who breathed out the Scriptures for us[18] and warmly surrounds us with His comfort when comfort is desired or urges us on to next steps of obedience when encouragement to that end is needed.[19] He often accomplishes His work through what He urges others to do for us.

It is not saying too much to say that our Christian lives are lived completely dependent upon the presence and power of the Holy Spirit. Our ignorance of this impoverishes our devotion. Unaware of the Spirit's pervasive work we claim too much credit for ourselves for the growth and progress we see in our lives. And in forgetting the gift the Holy Spirit is and the power He brings, we fail to lean on Him for help in times of need.

A friend for a while attended a Pentecostal church, a church community that pays special attention to the work and power of the Holy Spirit. It was a wonderful church, but my friend came to feel that while he heard a great deal about the power of God, as he should have, he longed to hear more about the grace of God. The irony of this, of

---

to establish each of these points by single verse references when full books could be written on any of them.

16 John 16:7-11; Galatians 5:22, 23; Philippians 1:6.

17 Romans 8:26, 27.

18 2 Timothy 3:16; 2 Peter 1:21.

19 John 16:6, 7.

course, is that the Holy Spirit is the agent of both power and grace. A possibly greater and sadder irony is that one can be in a Reformed or otherwise non-Pentecostal church and fail to hear about, and to lean upon, the power of God, the power mediated through and poured upon His Church by the Holy Spirit.

May we be those knowing both the power and the grace of God, both of which are made available to us by His Holy Spirit.

12

Teach Us to Pray

Woodworking is my diversion. I have a shop with tools I've collected over the years and, given the opportunity—all too rare—I can lose myself there and sometimes emerge with something useful, and perhaps beautiful. It is my delight.

But I can't tell you how I came to be a woodworker. I didn't really *start*. I did not resolve to become a woodworker. I did not learn by reading books or watching YouTube videos. My dad was a carpenter, so I was probably pounding nails into boards before I went to school. Woodworking is just something I've always done.

Having addressed the Word and the sacraments as means of grace, the Catechism turns to prayer, and so that will concern us now. But is prayer a learned skill for the Christian? Is it a mystery for us that needs to be unlocked by attending a class or watching a how-to video? I don't think so. If you are a Christian, you pray. You already pray. Like my woodworking, you do it. It is something you've always done. Even if your prayer has only been 'God, help me!', you pray. To be a Christian is to pray.

There came a time, though, when my dad taught the child driving nails into boards how to use that skill to frame a house. Later he showed me how to install baseboard, door trim, and chair rails to make the house beautiful. He nurtured an impulse and honed it in the direction of beauty. The Catechism sets out to nurture our impulse to pray and to hone it in a direction of beauty using a prayer that Jesus taught His disciples, a prayer known to us as the Lord's Prayer.

'You should pray more!', a voice whispers in our ears. Perhaps that is true, but that voice will not move us to pray. Delight in prayer will. There came a time in my life where I could spend an entire day installing trim in a house because I delighted in it. I now look for opportunities to disappear into my shop.

Lack of prayer is less a lack of discipline as it is a lack of appreciation for the delight that prayer can be. The Catechism, building on Jesus' own teaching on prayer, aims to restore that delight.[1]

59 Prayer

> Q. 98. What is prayer?
> A. Prayer is an offering up of our desires unto God, for things agreeable to his will, in the name of Christ, with confession of our sins, and thankful acknowledgment of his mercies.

---

1   As I learned from my dad, so we, too, learn prayer from the wise who have gone before us. Two books in particular have been a great help to me. Both of these will find further mention in these studies. Paul Miller's *A Praying Life: Connecting with God in a Distracting World* (United States: NavPress, 2009) is the most practical and wise guide I have found. David Crump's *Knocking on Heaven's Door: A New Testament Theology of Petitionary Prayer* (United States: Baker Academic, 2006) is a sound and refreshingly realistic consideration of what prayer, as it is taught in the New Testament, really is. Both books made me want to pray.

The life of prayer is full of danger. Hope, certainly, surrounds prayer. But the dangers are real and need to be acknowledged at the outset.

I remember being taught as a child that God would give me what I asked for if I prayed for it. So, for some reason, I prayed for a tractor. I did not get my tractor. What I did get was a lifetime of questions about prayer.

These questions haunt many who pray and expose the dangers that arise. Some pray earnestly for the healing of a loved one who is, in the end, not healed. Others pray for jobs that do not materialize or friendships that evaporate. Prayer raises hopes that seem to be dashed, leading some to stop praying or to stop believing in God or His goodness. It leads some to blame themselves for not praying right or having sufficient faith.

Prayer is dangerous, and it is made dangerous by focusing not on the opportunity it is but on the mystery of God's response. The Catechism's wonderful definition of prayer simply invites us to offer up our desires to God. Prayer is the opportunity to speak our heart to God. Prayer is not a way to extract things from God. It is an invitation to pour out our hearts before Him.

To focus on the results can create quite a fog. To soften the struggle, qualifiers are offered. 'God answers every prayer; sometimes the answer is, "No,"' we are told. Or, 'Prayer is not intended to change God, but to change us.' Though well-intentioned and in certain ways true, such qualifiers feel trite and unhelpful. Their net effect can strip from the Christian any real hope in prayer and in God Himself.

Further, they seem to dismiss the bold claims for prayer that Jesus Himself made.[2] His words embolden us to ask things of a God who cares, who listens, and who desires to give to us what we ask. And the fact that God on occasion did not give even to Jesus what He asked did not seem to unsettle Jesus or make Him even less bold.

Jesus prayed boldly in the Garden of Gethsemane that He be given a path other than that which led through the cross.[3] That was His heart's desire. Yes, He submitted His prayer to the will of His Father, believing that His Father was wise and good. But that did not seem to lessen the intensity and hopefullness of His prayer. He does not shrink back from prayer or qualify His prayer. He prayed earnestly expressing His deepest and true desires, revealing that what He sought in prayer He believed God could give.

sincere intensity

Yes, God does sometimes say, 'No,' as He did with Jesus. But what we are to learn from this incident in the life of Jesus has nothing to do with what God does with our prayers and everything to do with praying itself. Like Jesus we are permitted as children to ask anything. We are encouraged to honestly and fervently let our requests and desires and hearts be known. Prayer is not to be reduced to an exercise of contemplation or an act of meditation. It is

---

2   A few examples:
    'Ask, and it will be given to you; seek, and you will find; knock, and it will be opened to you' (Matt. 7:7).
    'And whatever you ask in prayer, you will receive, if you have faith' (Matt. 21:22).
    'If you ask me anything in my name, I will do it' (John 14:14).

3   'And going a little farther he fell on his face and prayed, saying, "My Father, if it be possible, let this cup pass from me; nevertheless, not as I will, but as you will"' (Matt. 26:39).

not simply a spiritual discipline that should occupy a place in the Christian's daily walk so that we might be changed. Prayer is real. It is an honest, raw cry to God for things that our heart is saying that we, or those we love, need and which we earnestly desire. We ought never get bogged down over whether God will or will not answer, or presume to explain Him or qualify Him. His ways are not what should concern us in prayer. Rather, what should concern us is what we are permitted and indeed *encouraged*, to lay before God. He wants to hear our most outrageous desires. Even if that is for a tractor. Or a spouse. Or another day of life.

David Crump—whose book on prayer, *Knocking on Heaven's Door*,[4] I mentioned in this chapter's introduction—was asked by a conference organizer what was the most important thing he had learned from his study of prayer. His answer was, 'Though I still struggle with it, I have learned to believe that God is always faithful.'[5] So much, he went on to say, hangs on those words.

God is faithful. That's all we need to know. He'll do the right thing. His heart is to hear the pleas of His children. Don't try to figure God out. Just pray. Just ask. Just trust God to do the right thing. And in this, prayer will be less dangerous and more hopeful.

---

4   David Crump, *Knocking on Heaven's Door: A New Testament Theology of Petitionary Prayer* (United States: Baker Academic, 2006).

5   From personal correspondence.

60 A RULE FOR PRAYER

> Q. 99. What rule has God given for our direction in prayer?
> A. The whole Word of God is of use to direct us in prayer; but the special rule of direction is that form of prayer which Christ taught his disciples, commonly called the Lord's Prayer.

Prayer is talking to God as freely as we talk to a friend or to a loved one. It is an 'offering up of our desires unto God' as we discussed in the last section. Such freedom seems oddly constrained when we then begin to talk about a 'rule' which God has given 'for our direction in prayer.' Prayer should be free and not bound by rules, we protest. Such a protest is well taken, but misdirected.

The word 'rule' does at times refer to a strict law which is not to be violated. It is a rule that a golfer not move his ball to a more favorable placement, for example. But 'rule' can also be understood as a standard by which we measure an action. A 'ruler' is a tool we use to compare the length of an object to a standard. A 'rule' in this sense is a pattern by which other things are shaped. When Jesus' disciples asked Jesus, 'Lord, teach us to pray,'[6] Jesus responded in a way that suggests both connotations of 'rule' are to some degree true.

In Luke, Jesus answers saying, 'When you pray, say…'[7] and follows with the words we commonly call the Lord's

6 Luke 11:1.
7 Luke 11:2.

Prayer. This sounds like a law: 'Here are the words to use when you pray.' And so the Church has faithfully used these words over the centuries. Christians from all traditions have been taught to pray using these very words. Consequently, when they gather and pray this prayer, they pray these words with almost no deviation and, therefore, experience a profound unity. It is right to pray in *just* this way with *just* these words.

And yet at the same time, these words are given not to constrain the language of prayer, but to shape the direction and rhythm of prayer. Giving similar teaching on prayer in a different context, Jesus introduces the language of the Lord's Prayer by telling His disciples to 'pray then like this....'[8] Here the prayer is offered as a pattern by which our words in prayer are guided. Jesus leads us down the broad categories, or petitions, which are to characterize our prayers and then sets us free to pray 'like this.'

In early twentieth-century Paris many American artists, later to achieve renown on their own, could be found in the Louvre, literally copying the masters found there.[9] Each of these artists would later paint with their own style and artistic touch. But they learned first by attending to the models of the masters who had preceded them.

When we similarly copy Jesus, attending to the model He gives as our master, we are learning more than the words to use in prayer. By letting His prayer guide us, letting it be our rule, His prayer shapes the very desires we bring in prayer. To be guided by the petitions of the Lord's Prayer is

8   Matthew 6:9.

9   David McCullough, *The Greater Journey: Americans in Paris* (United States: Simon & Schuster, 2011).

to have our longings and our loves massaged in the direction of the heart of God. As artists in the Louvre would begin to see with the eyes of Rembrandt or da Vinci, shaping our prayers by the petitions of this prayer invites us to see with the eyes of Jesus in all our praying.

When we pray, we offer our desires up to God, freely and sometimes passionately. Shaped by this rule, our prayers will be more wise and more reflective of the heart of God and therefore, in the end, more hopeful and satisfying.

61 PRAYER TO A FATHER

> Q. 100. What does the preface of the Lord's Prayer teach us?
> A. The preface of the Lord's Prayer, which is,
> **Our Father which art in heaven,**
> teaches us to draw near to God with all holy reverence and confidence, as children to a father able and ready to help us; and that we should pray with and for others.

In the Lord's Prayer Jesus leads us to speak to God as He has spoken to God—as Father. Prayer, we learn, is an act by which children bring their needs to a loving father. No doubt Jesus knew there were such things as bad fathers and absent fathers. He uses this imagery anyway, because we all know instinctively what a father is to be. Jesus encourages us to pray to God in heaven as a perfect father, one who represents all that a father ought to be.

Good fathers have hearts that are inclined to the good of their children. Children implicitly know when they need something that Dad (or Mom!) is the one to ask. They have no other resource. If Mom or Dad can't supply it, none can. Children don't hold back with good fathers. They know they can ask anything. They know that they will not get all they ask, and as frustrating as that is, they take comfort in knowing that their father still loves them. A father is available to his children. He is strong and safe and generous. This is how we are to see our God, and this is the way we are to pray to Him.

To pray in any other way loses the heart of prayer.

If we pray to God as a judge, then we must prove ourselves worthy of His positive response. A judge, unlike a father, keeps us at a distance. We can appeal to him, yes, but only on his schedule. We can't burst into his chambers as we can burst in on our father. With a judge we must prove our worth and try to curry his favor to earn a hearing for our prayers. Such considerations, necessary before a judge, are ridiculous before a good father.

If, on the other hand, God is merely a force or power, then He becomes one whom we must manipulate to get our desires. We need to be concerned that we align our prayers aright to properly invoke the power of the force. We will need to say the right words in the right order in the right way at the right time. God becomes little more than a magical vending machine into which we need to deposit the proper currency. Such a god has no interest in us, nor we in it.

A father, however, can hear what we mean even when our words are lost under a flood of tears or confused in a jumble of misdirected desires. A good father, unlike a judge or force, loves the child who draws near to him and is ever inclined to listen to what is meant even when buried in a torrent of confused words. It is a joy to realize that we pray to a heavenly Father.

And we pray to Him together. When Jesus teaches us to pray to 'Our' (plural) Father He reminds us that it is good to pray with others. This is formally accomplished in things like public worship. But in informal contexts, too, we need to pray for and with one another.

A few years ago at a time of deep personal distress I was sitting on a wall outside a hospital unable to hold back tears born of fear and confusion. A woman walked over to me and asked how I was doing, and I tried, cautiously, to tell her. Soon, she asked, 'May I pray with you?' The prayer of this Pentecostal woman was far different than any prayer this careful Presbyterian pastor would pray, but it was right and it was good and it was to the one who is my Father and hers. We prayed to our Father, and as children bursting in upon Him, we were welcome. We pray as children to a good and loving Father.

62 Prayer's Chief End

Q. 101. What do we pray for in the first petition?
A. In the first petition, which is,
Hallowed be your name,
we pray that God would enable us and others to glorify him in all that whereby he makes himself known; and that he would dispose all things to his own glory.

In the 2009 movie *Taken*, Liam Neeson plays a retired CIA agent whose daughter is kidnapped by a ring of human traffickers. It is a loud and violent movie in which Neeson destroys half of Paris (it seems) in order to find and win his daughter's release. Clearly his daughter mattered to him. She was sacred to him. In a sense, she was holy.

Those things which matter to us, those things we protect and defend, those things we guard and treasure, these are the things sacred to us. Understandably our children fall into that category. Often, certain possessions or freedoms are things we will protect. In certain cultures, certain animals are sacred and in others certain days and places. Things we value rightly or wrongly become the holy things we care most about and the things we protect.

Jesus teaches us to begin our prayers acknowledging that of all those things that might matter to us, God is to be supreme. God is the most holy and most sacred focus of our adoration. This is the central theme that must shape our prayers. God's glory is to be the chief end of our prayers as it is of our lives.[10] God alone is the one whose name is glorious and it is His name, His person, whom we should 'hallow' (revere or make holy) in all we do and desire. We are to make this our prayer because we, like all others, too easily displace Him from this central position of glory.

To begin prayer with this desire reminds us that it is only when God our Father occupies this central, sacred place of worship that everything else—family, freedom, and possessions—becomes properly ordered. This nurtures the

---

10 See Q/A 1.

desire in us, no matter what we seek from God, that He would receive that proper supremacy. Nothing, even the good things we ask for, should supplant Him there.

Life misfires because we, like Adam, tend to hallow the wrong things. To pray 'hallowed be your name' orients our prayers and our lives properly to the way things are meant to be. Even Jesus, in distress, hallowed His Father's name by submitting His very life in prayer to His Father's wisdom.[11]

It is proper that our prayers be filled with our wants. We pray for daily bread and for deliverance from evil, for new jobs and for a loving spouse. These wants, when sought as Jesus here teaches, will be shaded in the direction of the ultimate and sacred desire that God's glory would be served. Only then will things be the way they are meant to be, and ultimately only then will we find our full and complete happiness.

And we won't have to destroy Paris, or our or others' lives, to find it.

63 PRAYER AND THE KINGDOM

> Q. 102. What do we pray for in the second petition?
> A. In the second petition, which is,
> **Your kingdom come,**
> we pray that Satan's kingdom may be destroyed; and that the kingdom of grace may be advanced, ourselves and others brought into it, and kept in it; and that the kingdom of glory may be hastened.

3 things

---

11 'And he said, "Abba, Father, all things are possible for you. Remove this cup from me. Yet not what I will, but what you will"' (Mark 14:36).

in this age, citizens
in the age to come, New Heavens + New Earth

In a small box near where I write are dozens of 3x5 index cards. On the front of these cards are the names of the people I know. Here are the names of family, of church members, of friends, and of colleagues in ministry. On the back of these cards I have written the needs for which I pray.[12] Were you to glance at these, you would discover a host of very local and very mundane needs. Most of us pray for ordinary and personal things like this. We pray for friends' sorrows to be lifted and for siblings' surgeries to be successful. We ask for wisdom to choose between two jobs or two suitors. We pray for personal injustice to be remedied and for a distant missionary to be blessed. Such prayers and many more like them are proper and should be continued and multiplied.

These are prayers we pray out of our own need and out of a concern for our friends. But on another level they are at the same time prayers for the winning of a war. Our prayers express the desire that Christ's kingdom would come.

This world is God's good creation fallen under the influence of darkness. Under the dominion of Satan, things in this world are not as they ought to be. He attacks all that is good and right and seeks to make ugly what God created beautiful. He acts in whatever way he can to disrupt, deface, and diminish God's good creation.

When Christ became man He invaded this occupied territory, and His death on the cross was His victory over the usurper. His resurrection from the dead was a vindication of His victory and His ascension to heaven was His coronation. Jesus

---

12 Again, I commend to you Paul Miller's book, *A Praying Life*, from which this practice was learned.

is the rightful king of this world, and wherever His rule is not acknowledged is territory yet to be brought into submission.

Satan does not relinquish his hold easily. Wherever temptation finds a foothold is where Satan seeks to retain influence. He revels in injustice and ignorance, in hypocrisy and disease, in hatred and gossip. When we pray against any of these things, we are not just praying that these sad things would come untrue,[13] but also that the power and grasp of Satan would be undone by the power of God and that the kingdom of Christ, God's Son, would come.

Our prayers are weapons in this great unfolding of events. We pray most often implicitly, and sometimes explicitly, that Christ's kingdom of grace, where He is known and served, might be advanced and that everything good that could happen to expand Christ's influence would in fact come to pass. In praying against the world's brokenness and for things to be as they are supposed to be, we are looking forward to the ultimate expression of Christ's kingdom with His return and the inauguration of eternity. To pray for the coming of the kingdom is to pray, ultimately, 'Come, Lord Jesus'[14] with the heart's desire that '…the earth will be filled with the glory of the knowledge of the Lord as the waters cover the sea.'[15]

Our prayers are *not* insignificant no matter how mundane they appear to us. Whether we are praying simply for the

---

13 As J. R. R. Tolkien's Sam Gamgee so memorably envisioned the future in *The Lord of the Rings: The Return of the King*: 'Gandalf! I thought you were dead! But then I thought I was dead myself. Is everything sad going to come untrue? What's happened to the world?' (United States: Houghton Mifflin Company, 1994), p. 930.

14 Revelation 22:20.

15 Habbakuk 2:14.

healing of our beloved friend or directly for the salvation of the nations, we are praying in the midst of a war for the victory of our King. Those requests scribbled on the backs of 3x5 cards are in fact battle objectives for the sake of the kingdom of God. If anything, knowing this makes our prayers more pointed, more urgent, and more passionate. There is a cosmic character to our prayers that we often forget.

To pray with this desire, 'your kingdom come,' is to say that we believe that something better than the way things are is not only possible but certain. It encourages us to pray with more confidence, for the kingdom that will come and will never disappear.

64 PRAYER AND GOD'S WILL

> Q. 103. What do we pray for in the third petition?
> A. In the third petition, which is,
> **Your will be done in earth, as it is in heaven,**
> we pray that God, by his grace, would make us able and willing to know, obey and submit to his will in all things, as the angels do in heaven.

Jesus was alone with God in the garden. Though the disciples were nearby, Jesus was conscious of only being alone with His Father. He saw the chasm ahead of Him that was the cross, and in His humanity it was terrifying to consider. He prayed: 'Father, if you are willing, remove this cup from me.'[16] He was pleading with His Father that some other way be found, some other less terrifying path be opened. So agonizing was His pleading that it is said He sweated drops of blood.

He asked God to change His path, but He did so with a heart of willing submission. He was content to submit His earnest pleas to the absolute and limitless wisdom of God. 'Nevertheless,' He prayed, 'not my will, but yours, be done.'[17] He prayed as He had previously taught His disciples to pray, 'Your will be done on earth as it is in heaven.'[18] He prayed with a heart fully submissive to the purposes of His Father. The drops of blood He sweated reveal that this was no easy place to reach. His calm commitment after He prayed reveals that this is a place of peace we long to reach.

We have made the point that to ask God for whatever our hearts desire is the privilege of children before their Father.[19] But we do not ask as spoiled children, expecting that our Father is therefore obligated to give us everything we ask. God does not always take the hard things away. We are to pray with the words 'your will be done' on our lips or not far from our minds, knowing that ultimately God is wise and knows our need better than we do. Only this frame of mind is sufficient to breed contentment and peace in our prayers. To be willing to know and submit to His will is the nature

---

16 Luke 22:42a.

17 Luke 22:42b.

18 Matthew 6:10.

19 '…do not be anxious about anything, but in everything by prayer and supplication with thanksgiving let your requests be made known to God' (Phil. 4:6).

of the perfect joy of heaven. It is not easy to adopt such an attitude. To reach it is a grace for which we pray.

When pastor and scholar James Montgomery Boice announced to his Philadelphia congregation that he had liver cancer, he and they knew that apart from God intervening, his life was coming to a premature end. And yet he said, 'God is in charge. When things like this come into our lives, they are not accidental. It's not as if God somehow forgot what was going on, and something bad slipped by…. God does everything according to his will.'[20] The theology behind this we have covered in these pages. Prayer often reveals our theology in its richest application.

Dr Boice went on to remind his congregation, 'God is not only the one who is in charge; God is also good. Everything He does is good.'[21] No doubt he and his congregation were praying for his healing. And yet, they prayed submissive to the good and perfect will of God. They did not simply accept stoically that God's will would be done. They desired it (as hard as that must have been) because they believed God to be good.

Dr Boice concluded with this, 'If God does something in your life, would you change it? If you'd change it, you'd make it worse. It wouldn't be as good. So that's the way we want to accept it and move forward, and who knows what God will do?'[22]

---

20 Read by Dr Boice to the congregation of Tenth Presbyterian Church, Philadelphia, on May 7, 2000. Quoted here and elsewhere: https://www.tenth.org/resource-library/sermons/attaining-maturity, accessed 12/30/2019.
21 ibid.
22 ibid.

Who knows what God will do? This is the expectant wonder fueled by praying that God's will would be done. In the end, Jesus had to drink the agonizing cup He'd asked to avoid. What would God do with this? He gave us life.

When we pray that His will be done in our own lives, and that we might joyfully receive whatever that will may be, who knows what God will do? We don't. But we do know He is good and that He is our Father, and when we are alone with Him that is what matters most.

65 PRAYER FOR DAILY NEEDS

> Q. 104. What do we pray for in the fourth petition?
> A. In the fourth petition, which is,
> **Give us this day our daily bread,**
> we pray that of God's free gift we may receive a competent portion of the good things of this life, and enjoy his blessing with them.

Many of the children at the school where my niece works are on the autistic spectrum and come from troubled homes. Consequently, my niece reports, many hoard their food. Even though they are not allowed to take it home, they try. The meals that they get at school are likely the only food upon which they can rely on any given day. Tomorrow is so uncertain that they don't want to let go of what they have today. My niece's heart breaks for these little children.

We see this as tragic, as we should. But we should also see it as a mirror into our own troubled relationship with tomorrow. We live our lives with an eye upon an uncertain tomorrow. We therefore work hard, set our plans, exercise our creativity, and in many cases hoard what we have, believing that if we don't, we will have nothing when the sun rises. If we are going to have the good things we desire, then we must work for them.

It was this sense of self-reliance coupled with uncertainty about tomorrow that led some Israelites in their desert wanderings to gather extra manna to keep overnight.[23] We say it is wise to plan for a rainy day, and it is, of course. But our planning can become a controlling commitment to self-dependence. Jesus here teaches us to pray in such a way that reminds us, when all the plans are executed and the goals achieved, it is really God on whom we depend for those good things we seek.

Most of us I suspect cannot identify with the hunger and fear experienced by my niece's students. But without a sense of need, we can easily lose a sense of wonder. We see the food on our table as coming from the grocery and not from God. Rather than celebrating a meal as His gift, we grumble that the pizza guy is late. Dependent, as we think, only on ourselves, we are less likely to marvel over what we have. And for this we are the poorer.

---

23 In Exodus 16 we learn that the food God gave to the Israelites in the desert every night, the manna, would spoil if any tried to gather extra and store it for the next day. This is the picture behind Jesus' language of 'daily' bread. It would be new and fresh every morning, but only every morning.

In contrast, Jesus teaches all—poor fishermen and wealthy tax collectors,[24] servers at the local diner and retired CEOs—to pray for their daily provision. In so doing he trains us all to look to our Father for all that we need for each day. Praying this prayer faithfully changes how we look at tomorrow and how we look at things, those portions of the good life we have.

We have a troubled relationship with things. We want more than we need, and we tie our happiness to what we have. God blesses us with wonderfully good things which we see not simply as good but necessary. Our hearts' devotion moves from the giver to the gift. We center our joy in the thing we have and not the one who gave it. This prayer challenges us to enjoy the provision without losing sight of the provider.

When Job, a rich and well-blessed man, lost all his things he said: 'The LORD gave, and the LORD has taken away; blessed be the name of the LORD.'[25] The Apostle Paul, whose fortunes often changed, was able to confess: 'I have learned in whatever situation I am to be content.'[26] Such attitudes of faithful contentment grow from seeing all we have as a gift, as daily bread given to us by a giver who never fails us.

We who hoard, whether autistic kindergarteners, desert wanderers, or suburban professionals, will find joy when we can trust another, God, to bear the responsibility for tomorrow. To that end, we look to Him for our daily bread.

---

24 His twelve closest followers, to whom this prayer was taught, came from different economic classes.

25 Job 1:21.

26 Philippians 4:11.

66 PRAYER FOR FORGIVENESS

> Q. 105. What do we pray for in the fifth petition?
> A. In the fifth petition, which is,
>
> **And forgive us our debts, as we forgive our debtors,[27]**
>
> we pray that God, for Christ's sake, would freely pardon all our sins; which we are the rather encouraged to ask, because by his grace we are enabled from the heart to forgive others.

Anne Lamott's 2012 book, *Help, Thanks, Wow: The Three Essential Prayers,*[28] falls one prayer short of completeness. According to Jesus there is in fact a fourth essential prayer, 'I'm sorry.' Our prayers are to include an admission of our wrongdoing and a heartfelt desire for God's forgiveness.

But this puzzles us. Why would a Christian be expected to pray this? We have seen how Jesus gave His life for our justification and redeemed us from the curse of the law.[29] He has forgiven us all our sins past, present, and future through His death on the cross. It would seem that to ask Him for the forgiveness He has already given us would be to

---

27 Some traditions speak here of 'trespasses' and 'those who trespass against us' in the place of 'debts' and 'debtors.' The meaning is the same. The words speak of sins and those who commit them.

28 Anne Lamott, *Help, Thanks, Wow: The Three Essential Prayers* (United States: Riverhead Books, 2012).

29 'Christ redeemed us from the curse of the law by becoming a curse for us—for it is written, "Cursed is everyone who is hanged on a tree"' (Gal. 3:13).

discount all of this. To confess sin repeatedly seems, at best, unnecessarily redundant.

And yet Jesus expects us to do so, knowing that the giving and accepting of forgiveness is at the heart of any vital relationship.

We pray, as we have said, as children to our Father. But try as we might to be obedient children, we fail. We sin against Him and against others. Yes, that sin is forgiven, and yes, that sin was paid for at the cross. Our status is not changed. We who are children continue to be children.

Nevertheless, the relationship is strained. By our sin we feel estranged from God. Our feelings of guilt introduce a sense of separation. As children we need to go to our Father, tell Him our wrong, and ask for the forgiveness we know He is able and willing to give. In our confession we do not change our relationship with God, but we do renew and restore it.

There are times I travel long distances to meet someone only to have them cancel at the last minute. This infuriates and frustrates me. I still love the person who has canceled. I'm still his friend. Our relationship will continue. But there is still a tension introduced into the relationship. For all again to be well between us, it is good that he tell me that he is sorry. It is good that he asks me for forgiveness. The forgiveness is ready and easily given, but the transaction is necessary. Wrong disrupts a relationship. Saying 'I'm sorry' and hearing 'I forgive you' opens the path of healing.

In this spirit we confess our sin to God and He forgives us. And it is in this same spirit that we are to forgive others. To forgive others can be hard, but it is more easily done when we know that we ourselves have been freely pardoned by a holy God. The relationship between our confession to God and our forgiveness of others is a tight one.

The heart of a Christian's gospel hope is that she is forgiven by the atoning work of Jesus Christ on the cross, not her ability to confess. Christians will die with many sins unconfessed, but with all sins pardoned. And yet, to regularly confess the sins of which we are aware is not to descend into morbid introspection, but it is to live in a place of consistent joy. By it we are relieved of our guilt and reminded that we are our Father's beloved children.

At the end of the day Lamott has this going for her with her abbreviated catalog of prayers. To our 'I'm sorry,' God says, 'I know. I forgive you.' To this we have no other response but to say, 'Wow. Thanks. Help me show this grace to others.'

67 Prayer for Steadiness

Q. 106. What do we pray for in the sixth petition?
A. In the sixth petition, which is,
And lead us not into temptation, but deliver us from evil,
we pray that God would either keep us from being tempted to sin, or support and deliver us when we are tempted.

The Christian life can be hard. We live it, as the eighteenth-century hymn writer John Newton put it, through many dangers, toils, and snares.[30] And so it is good when we pray to ask God to steer us clear of those dangers and snares, that He would lead us around and away from temptation, and save us from the evil this world uses to distract us.

Those who have lived any amount of time as Christians know that though the Christian life can be full of delight and refreshment, it can at times be disorienting and tough. Our way can become confused, and we can weary of the journey. The world's allure and the devil's schemes tempt us to be unfaithful to God or, when faithful, to look with contemptuous pride on others. We need God's constant care to steady us.

In teaching us to pray this way, Jesus in no way means to suggest that God tempts us. He is not the one we need fear. When I walk with a grandchild through the woods, she knows I will do her no harm. But she hopes, as well, that her grandfather will lead her clear of bears and snakes and other dangers. Our prayer is that God, our Father, would steer us in such a way that the dangers are few. To pray this is to desire steadiness in our walk, and steadfastness in our faithfullness. And it is to admit that we can do neither on our own.

Temptations to step away from the path abound and are rarely obvious. In John Bunyan's allegory *The Pilgrim's Progress*,[31] the hero Christian and his companion Hopeful, walking along one long and lonely stretch of road, spy a path

---

30   John Newton, 'Amazing Grace', *The Trinity Hymnal, Revised Edition*, #460.

31   Available online in various formats at https://www.gutenberg.org/ebooks/131. Many print editions exist. My favorite is John Bunyan, *The Pilgrim's Progress* (United States: Banner of Truth, 1977).

parallel to their own that looks far less arduous. They pass through a gate and take this new and easier path, straight into the arms of Giant Despair, the lord of Doubting Castle, from whose clutches they do not easily escape. Jesus would have us desire, and so pray, that God would lead us far away from such enticements that lead to our harm. We pray that we would have the strength to walk by when we do come close.[32] We want to be steady.

If we are given to anger, then it is good to ask God to protect us from too much harsh news too quickly, that the temptation to erupt might be lessened. If we are given to impulsive sexual behavior, then our prayer is that God would lead us away from those people or images whose sexual stimulation overwhelm our control. In praying that God would lead us away from temptation, we are praying that God would so guide our lives each day that nothing would come across our paths that would cause us to fall. We want to live steady, faithful Christian lives. For this, we need God's daily help.

We might look at the sinless life of Jesus and imagine that we could live the same way. We can't and we won't. Nevertheless it is good for us to know that He knew what it meant to be tempted. He is sympathetic to our weakness.[33] From this place of understanding He teaches us to pray that God will lead us away from temptation. And when we

---

32 'No temptation has overtaken you that is not common to man. God is faithful, and he will not let you be tempted beyond your ability, but with the temptation he will also provide the way of escape, that you may be able to endure it' (1 Cor. 10:13).

33 'For we do not have a high priest who is unable to sympathize with our weaknesses, but one who in every respect has been tempted as we are, yet without sin' (Heb. 4:15).

believe ourselves to be overwhelmed, He teaches us to ask God to confront and defeat the evil that is before us when we are too weak to lift a finger against it.

As Christians we want to live lives that forever and always give honor to our God. We pray that He will help steady us for this path, knowing that, as Newton continued: ''Tis grace has brought me safe thus far, and grace will lead me home.'[34]

68 ENCOURAGEMENT TO PRAYER

Q. 107. What does the conclusion of the Lord's Prayer teach us?

A. The conclusion of the Lord's Prayer, which is,

For yours is the kingdom, and the power, and the glory, forever, Amen,

teaches us to take our encouragement in prayer from God only, and in our prayers to praise him, ascribing kingdom, power and glory to him. And in testimony of our desire, and assurance to be heard, we say, Amen.

Barb and I visited a locally famous barbecue restaurant a number of years ago. It was her first visit. As we neared the end of our lunch, a distinguished looking man with graying hair and a warm smile stopped by our table and asked Barb what she thought of her meal. She expressed satisfaction, and he said, 'Have you tried the brisket?' She said that she had

---

34 John Newton, 'Amazing Grace', *The Trinity Hymnal, Revised Edition*, #460.

not. He said, 'Would you like to try some?' She hesitated, and so I answered for her, 'Yes, she would. Thank you.' When he went to get her some brisket I told her, 'When the owner of the restaurant offers you food, you take it.'

Barb did not know to whom she was speaking. I did. And knowing to whom we are speaking makes a great deal of difference.

We conclude our prayers, Jesus teaches, with a reminder of just who it is to whom we are speaking. The one before whom we bring our every care, from the seemingly petty ('daily bread') to the deeply profound ('thy kingdom'), is the Creator of all things. He rules all of reality with absolute authority. Everything conforms to His inexorable will and bends toward His unrivaled glory. The one with whom we are privileged to speak is, we have seen, 'infinite, eternal, and unchangeable in his being, wisdom, power, holiness, justice, goodness, and truth.'[35] We pray to one who is able to do all that we can ask or imagine.[36] His actions are limited by nothing other than His wisdom and glory. Through the cross He has shown Himself to be willing to go to unfathomable lengths to act on behalf of those He loves. When the owner of the universe encourages you to ask for whatever is on your heart to ask, you ask. It is a privilege we too often disparage and forget.

But does He do what we ask? Paul Miller suggests He does. He tells the insightful, if whimsical, anecdote regarding His mother, Rose Marie, a woman faithful in prayer. He asked her whether it would be appropriate to pray for a parking place in a crowded city, or whether such a request would

---

35   Q/A #4.

36   Ephesians 3:20.

be too trivial for God. Her response was, 'How else would you find a parking place?'[37] Thus have mature Christians throughout history testified. How else but by prayer do we come by anything?

The mystery of what constitutes answered prayer is not for us to unpack here. Some of us don't see such immediate answers and it puzzles us. It is enough, however, to know that He desires our good and desires us to ask. The one to whom we speak is in the end our Father and we are His children. Every Scripture passage on prayer suggests that He whose is the kingdom, the power, and the glory does in fact act upon the prayers of His children. The history of God's people, and God's Word itself, assure us that we are heard, and when heard, every request is given the deepest and greatest consideration.[38] In the light of these things, we are the wiser if we take every desire of our hearts to Him, in the confidence of His hearing us say, 'Amen.'

When the owner tells us to ask for what is in His power to give, we ask.

Our Father invites us to ask.

So, ask.

Amen.

---

37   Paul Miller, *A Praying Life*, p. 119.

38   'And this is the confidence that we have toward him, that if we ask anything according to his will he hears us. And if we know that he hears us in whatever we ask, we know that we have the requests that we have asked of him' (1 John 5:14-5).

Epilogue
The Final Word

We have come to the end of the Catechism, having thought about a great many things sublime and spectacular. We have confronted the nature of God and the glories of His salvation. We have celebrated the qualities with which God adorns the Christian's walk and the gifts He gives through the means of grace. We have made our way through the puzzle and promise of prayer. At this point you probably know a good deal more than you did when you started. That is gratifying to me, as it presumably would have been to the authors of the Catechism.

But it is not all. My desire for you is something greater than merely knowing more. It has been my desire that in coming to know *about* God you might long to *know* God. Knowing about Him, we hope, will move you to love Him and to live for Him, and ultimately to enjoy Him.

And so we end our studies where we began, by considering what it is we have worth living for.

69 That We Might Glorify and Enjoy the One Who Loves

> Q. 1. What is the chief end of man?
> A. Man's chief end is to glorify God, and to enjoy him forever.

What do we have that is worth living for? More than that we might know true things, the goal of the Catechism and those who wrote it is that we might pursue a true and worthy purpose. To glorify and enjoy God is that purpose.

When we let our lives be driven by less worthy things, by, for example, money or pleasure, or by accomplishment or acquisition, we very well may reach our goals but remain unsatisfied. Created as we are in the image of God, we are created for relationship with Him. It is love we long for. To know that we are loved is where we will find peace. Riches and acclaim are not the currency of love. Grace is. Many of us live frantic, disordered lives, seeking a love that we cannot earn. The Catechism, meanwhile, introduces us to a love that we have not earned, that we cannot buy, that we therefore can never lose, and that we are to enjoy.

David Brooks, author and *New York Times* columnist, reflected on what motivates people to large and passionate ambitions in his book *The Road to Character*.[1] He notes that when people discover that they are loved by a love that is

---

1   David Brooks, *The Road to Character* (United States: Random House, 2015).

unearned '...there is a great desire to go meet this love and reciprocate this gift.'[2] That is, when we find we are loved there is a strong desire to love in return. This is the very heart of historic Christianity, that undeserving sinners are loved with an incomprehensible, limitless, and unearned love. It is reasonable to say that the proper response to such love is to glorify the lover and to enjoy his love forever.

It is this that gives Christians something worth living for. The great passion for God that Christians have shown over the centuries has not been fueled by layers of obligation and duty but by a love for the one who had loved them. We love, the Apostle John says, because God *first* loved us.[3] When we find that we are loved, the world then opens up to us as a place to enjoy that love by showing our love to God in return, whether in the music we create, the families we nurture, the relationships we build, or the flowers we plant. We live for Him in all these things because we are loved by Him.

To find in His grace and love something worth living for is to find satisfaction in all that we do. To enjoy Him allows us to enjoy our work. We need not set about changing the world, as if we could. And we need not worry about wasting our lives, as if that were possible. The world is deeply impacted by legions of men and women living faithful and good lives in response to the love they have received.

We all have been touched and encouraged and moved by God's ordinary people living faithfully. May we live so as well, in the delightful enjoyment of the God who loves us. It does not matter whether the end of life leaves us wealthy

2   ibid., p. 207.

3   1 John 4:19.

and renowned or poor and obscure. We will have lived for the one who loved us and gave Himself for us, and that will be enough. The one thing that gives all else meaning is to know that we are loved by God.

To glorify and enjoy the one who loves us is, in the end, Westley,[4] what we got here that's worth living for.

To God be the glory.

> *Oh, the depth of the riches and wisdom and knowledge*
> *of God!*
> *How unsearchable are his judgments and how*
> *inscrutable his ways!*
> *'For who has known the mind of the Lord,*
> *or who has been his counselor?'*
> *'Or who has given a gift to him*
> *that he might be repaid?'*
> *For from him and through him*
> *and to him are all things.*
> *To him be glory forever.*
> *Amen.*[5]

---

4   The mostly dead Westley is the one to whom Miracle Max addresses the question with which we began these studies, all from the 1987 movie, *The Princess Bride.*

5   Romans 11:36-37.

Acknowledgements

This book began as a love story.

Tarrik, a newly-engaged, recent college graduate, wanted to grow in his understanding of his Christian faith. To that end his fiancée, Gabrielle, gave him a book of introductory theology which he and I attempted to study together. When that book failed to engage us, I decided to write this one.

For years faithful readers of my blog have urged me to write more, and the elders of the church I pastor, Covenant Presbyterian Church in Oviedo, Florida, have encouraged my calling in that direction.

The congregations of Hope Presbyterian Church in Bradenton, Florida, and Covenant in Oviedo, have challenged me with their questions and trusted me with their doubts. Their fingerprints here are everywhere.

Wilbur, the hero pig of E. B. White's *Charlotte's Web*, observes, 'It is not often that someone comes along who is a true friend and a good writer.' True that is, and I am blessed with four, B. J. Milgate, Mike Osborne, David Scotchie, and Roy Starling, all who encouraged me repeatedly in this work.

Carol Arnold underwrote the coffee that fueled this. Nate Espino reined in an originally incomprehensible structure. Larry Edison made sure I spoke to people who no longer use words like 'piety.' Stuart Heaton braced me for the mysterious world of publishing.

Dr. Kimberly Justice encouraged me to write and assured me that I was not crazy for wanting to do so. John Frame gave early suggestions and surprising encouragement. That Jerram Barrs would attach his name to my book is far more than I could have hoped. And Christian Focus Publications took a risk with me, an unknown author.

I have needed you all.

When I would announce, 'This stupid book is awful,' my children would come along and tell me that it was not awful and it was not stupid. They are a rich gift to a hopelessly needy father.

My wife, Barb, has seen many wild ideas come and go over our forty-two years, and she has laughed at none of them. For this project she never doubted my ability nor questioned its viability. Without her steady, loving presence, and her careful reading, this book would not exist. My love for her has grown, even when she insisted on commas where I did not want commas. That the sentences she marked as not making sense now do is only one part of her many contributions to this work. Words rarely escape me. They do here.

I have been given the opportunity by God to do something that brings me joy. Such a kindness this is. I am grateful to the One who has given me *something worth living for*.

This book, it seems, has always been a love story.

Also available from Christian Focus Publications…

100 Devotional Readings
on Union With Christ

HOW TO LIVE AN
'IN CHRIST' LIFE

KENNETH BERDING

ISBN 978-1-5271-0559-1

How to Live an 'In Christ' Life

100 Devotional Readings on Union with Christ

KENNETH BERDING

Everywhere we look in the letters of Paul we encounter 'in Christ.' But how many of us know why the Apostle Paul uses this expression—or ones like it—over and over again in his letters? What is so important about being in Christ? Is it possible that when Paul talks about inChristness, he is handing us a set of keys that will open up his letters and reveal what is most essential to living the Christian life? In these 100 devotionals, we discover why inChristness is so important and how to live an in-Christ life.

I cannot remember the last time I read a book on union with Christ and was so convicted that I stopped and prayed. Without compromising biblical and theological depth, Berding unveils the innumerable ways union with Christ makes a real difference in the Christian life.

Matthew Barrett
Associate Professor of Christian Theology, Midwestern Baptist Theological Seminary, Kansas City, Missouri

Christian Focus Publications

Our mission statement –

STAYING FAITHFUL
In dependence upon God we seek to impact the world
through literature faithful to His infallible Word, the Bible.
Our aim is to ensure that the Lord Jesus Christ is presented
as the only hope to obtain forgiveness of sin, live a useful life
and look forward to heaven with Him.

Our books are published in four imprints:

CHRISTIAN
FOCUS

Popular works including biographies, commentaries, basic
doctrine and Christian living.

CHRISTIAN
HERITAGE

Books representing some of the
best material from the rich heri-
tage of the church.

MENTOR

Books written at a level suitable
for Bible College and seminary
students, pastors, and other serious readers. The imprint includes
commentaries, doctrinal studies,
examination of current issues and
church history.

CF4•K

Children's books for quality Bible
teaching and for all age groups:
Sunday school curriculum, puzzle
and activity books; personal and family devotional titles, biographies and
inspirational stories – because you
are never too young to know Jesus!

Christian Focus Publications Ltd,
Geanies House, Fearn, Ross-shire,
IV20 1TW, Scotland, United Kingdom.
www.christianfocus.com